A GUIDE TO
RESEARCHING RAILWAYS
J A WELLS

ADDITIONAL PHOTOGRAPHY
by
KEN MORTON AND IAN S CARR

First Published in 2003 by
Powdene Publicity Ltd.,
Unit 17, St. Peter's Wharf,
Newcastle upon Tyne, NE6 1TZ.

© J A Wells and Powdene Publicity Ltd.

Printed by
NB Group

British Library Cataloguing in Publication Data

Wells, James Alan
A Guide to
Researching Railways

ISBN: 0 9544493 0 4

CONTENTS

Preface

PART ONE   THE BACKGROUND

ACKNOWLEDGEMENTS

Sincere thanks are expressed to the following for their co-operation:-

Aberdeen University, King's College
Bo'ness & Kinneil Railway
Bowes Railway
Bressingham Steam Museum
Cardiff Central Library
Cornwall County Record Office
Darlington Railway Centre & Museum
Hertfordshire County Record Office
Historical Model Railway Association
Industrial Railway Society
Liverpool Record Office
Locomotive Club of Great Britain
Narrow Gauge Railway Society
National Railway Museum Library
Northamptonshire County Record Office
North Eastern Railway Association
Northumberland County Library
Oxfordshire County Library
Public Record Office, Kew
Railway Correspondence & Travel Society
Railway Gazette
Railway Heritage Association
Railway Preservation Society of Ireland
Railway World
Scottish Tourist Board
Somerset County Library
Southern Education & Library Board
Southern Electric Group
Stait Photo, Morpeth
'Steam Railway' magazine
Virgin Trains

Special thanks also to: Mrs J Wells; and to John Batey,
Stewart Bonney and staff, Philip Brooks, Ian S Carr,
Malcolm Charlton, Mike Dimelow, Keith Goodaire,
Tom Johnson, George Mitcheson, Ken Morton, Derek Patten,
Desmond Walton, David A Wells and Mrs Ann Wilson.

PREFACE

Are you one of those people who would love to know more about railways but are not sure how to begin? You look round at the railway scene and are bewildered. Taking a train journey may make you ponder questions to which you do not know the answer. What do the initials EWS stand for? Why are there so many liveries? Why did I see a mainly black diesel locomotive with Loadhaul in large letters?

If you are in the right place at the right time you could see a train pounding along hauled by a steam locomotive and say to yourself, "What's this – a steam engine? I thought they went out 20-30 years ago!" You would be right, so what was it doing there? You may find it even more puzzling to come across a station where several clean locomotives are standing and one or two working with vintage coaches or wagons. Again, questions may bombard your brain, seeking answers. "I didn't know these things existed!" you may say – but they do.

You could, on the other hand, find a disused track bed and wonder which route it was on and why the line was closed. Maybe you are hoping to make a model and need to know where you can find out something about the original.

Railways are fascinating in their diversity. There are locomotives of many kinds it is true, but consider also the development of speed and comfort for passengers, goods wagons, signalling, designs of bridges, stations, and the preservation of artefacts. Bear in mind too the many secrets hidden in minute books and the huge range of documents.

This book is divided into three parts to put you on the right track. The first section takes you through the essential basic background of railways from the earliest days to the British Railways era, then into Privatisation. This is followed by more than twenty sources of information which include not only libraries, museums and heritage centres but also magazines, study groups, videos and private research. Part Three offers you a choice of subjects to study depending on your interests – a general overall picture of railways or the beginning of a more in-depth search for knowledge. Apart from the obvious choices such as the history of locomotives, narrow gauge lines or station architecture, there are topics like cigarette cards and postage stamps.

J A WELLS

A GUIDE TO
RESEARCHING RAILWAYS

PART ONE
THE BACKGROUND

Chapter One
MAKE WAY FOR THE IRON HORSE

Every year numerous Christmas cards portray colourful stage coaches with energetic horses, rotund and contented coachmen, excited passengers and wintery weather which, in spite of the cold, has everyone looking happy. Those cosy scenes however bear little relation to reality. Think instead of people who waited patiently at the roadside for a late-running coach, which then passed full. People inside were so cramped they could not extend their legs, and trying to change position was limited to a slight constricted shuffle. Those travelling on the outside with the luggage would have tried to find some comfort on the lurching coach, exposed to all weathers. There could have been excitement on a journey of, say, twenty hours – or fear. Imagine two inebriated coachmen racing each other, scaring passengers out of their wits; floods, broken wheels, and the risk of a highwayman demanding money or valuables!

Roads were under-developed and exorbitant prices were charged for the conveyance of goods by canal. Everything was geared to the pace of horses whereas what was urgently needed was faster and cheaper transport over greater distances. Later this would be provided by railways which were destined to make large towns where there had been only tiny villages, create massive industrial expansion, and within ten years bring about such a social revolution that jobs were created for many thousands of people.

Let us first of all turn the spotlight and look back at how it all began. It started with the insatiable demand for coal, miles away from coalfields. If a colliery was near a navigable river it was a comparatively simple matter to convey its product to sailing ships. Quite often, if the water was shallow, the coal had to be loaded first into keels and transferred to ships in deeper water. As the coal seams were worked out it was necessary to develop collieries further inland and to transport the coal to the loading point along narrow strips of land known as waggonways. For this the land owners were paid considerable sums of money in wayleaves.

Following heavy rain these routes were covered in mud making it extremely difficult for men and horses. To overcome this, and the ruts left when the ground dried out, baulks of timber were laid to make the passage of wheels easier. Horses were then able to move heavier loads.

The first recorded waggonway in Great Britain ran from pits at Strelley to Wollaton, near Nottingham, about two miles. It was built under the direction of Huntington Beaumont in 1603-04. He then moved to Bedlington in Northumberland, where he rented collieries from the Bishop of Durham, and laid wooden waggonways to a small staith on the river Blyth. 21,571 tons of coal were shipped from there in 1609.

Remains of wooden 4ft 2in gauge waggonway excavated at former colliery site near Fencehouses and believed to date from c.1780, being covered by sheeting and small coal on 29 March 1996 – pending a decision as to its future. (Ian S Carr)

Wooden rails could soon be damaged by wheels so to give some protection from wear and tear thin iron plates were fixed on top of them in 1716 or earlier. These were liable to fracture, or the wood underneath them rot, so thicker plates were gradually introduced. These were laid by platelayers, a railway term widely used until the 1980s. In some areas these plates were four inches broad, 1¹/₄ inches thick and five feet in length. They proved very successful and hard wearing but cart wheels coming off the track were a constant problem until metal flanges were fitted. Experience showed that a flange on the wheels themselves was more effective. Cast iron wheels were made at Coalbrookdale in Shropshire from 1729.

Many collieries began using fish-bellied rails, so named because their lower edge was shaped like the underside of a fish. In October 1820 an improved method of rolling longer wrought iron rails was patented by John Birkinshaw of Bedlington Iron Works. These were used in great quantities not only by collieries but by railways as they developed throughout the country.

The first locomotive to run on rails was built in England by Richard Trevithick in 1802. Two years later he built another one which weighed five tons and worked briefly in an iron works in south Wales. On its first run of nine miles it hauled ten tons of iron (plus about 70 people who had jumped on the trucks) and won a bet of 500 guineas for its owner! Unfortunately it broke many rails. Richard Trevithick's observation that when the engine was moving the exhaust from the chimney made the fire burn more fiercely was embodied into the design of nearly every steam locomotive thereafter.

In 1812 Messrs Fenton, Murray and Wood built successful steam locomotives for use at Middleton colliery near Leeds. These worked on a rack-rail system where semi-circular lugs on one side of the rails were engaged by a toothed wheel on the locomotive in the belief that smooth wheels would not grip smooth rails even on the level. On the contrary, experiments carried out by William Hedley, viewer (i.e. colliery manager) at Wylam in Northumberland, proved conclusively that smooth wheels would run satisfactorily provided the weight of the locomotive was related to the load it was expected to pull. Three of his machines – *Puffing Billy* (circa 1813), *Wylam Dilly* and *Lady Mary* – shared the work at the colliery. 'Billy', as it was affectionately known by the locals, was a familiar sight for 48 years, hauling loads of 50 tons at six miles per hour. Wylam has a unique distinction in that other railway pioneers were born there or lived nearby – Nicholas Wood (1795-1865), Timothy Hackworth (1786-1850) and, most famous of all, George Stephenson (1781-1848).

As enginewright at Killingworth colliery just north east of Newcastle upon Tyne, George Stephenson produced his first locomotive in July 1814. *Blücher,* as it was called, was similar to the Middleton engines but without the rack system. Working closely with Nicholas Wood, the viewer, George Stephenson carried out numerous experiments and introduced the best results into about sixteen engines built at Killingworth. In 1822 one of them was used to demonstrate to curious visitors – and potential customers – how it could move twenty loaded waggons "with the utmost facility". This would save the labours of many men and horses. A loco built for Hetton colliery in County Durham circa 1820 survived until 1908.

The Hetton Colliery 0-4-0 locomotive was brought on a low-loader to stand outside George Stephenson's birthplace at North Wylam on 8 August 1975 for a Stephenson Day Fete. (Ian S Carr)

It was of course the railway between Stockton and Darlington in 1825 which really made the Stephensons' name in the north east. George and his son Robert had surveyed and supervised the building of this line which was the first in the world for public transport where steam locomotives would be used other than on colliery systems. The gauge was 4 feet 8$\frac{1}{2}$ inches, the same as at Killingworth, and no less than four-fifths of the track was from Bedlington Iron Works. For the momentous opening *Locomotion* number 1 was built at the works of Robert Stephenson in Newcastle. Its four wheels were joined in pairs on each side by coupling rods to give better adhesion.

Word spread like a forest fire in a wind as the opening day drew near. On the day itself enormous crowds swarmed around the tracks: the excited and curious, the unsure or worried, the cynical and those who were antagonistic. The little engine excelled itself, hauling six waggons of coal or flour, a coach for directors and proprietors, 21 waggons into which at least 450 people were crammed, and finally another six waggons. After the official opening rates of carriage were progressively reduced from five (old) pence to one-fifth of a penny; mineral charges dropped from seven pence to $1^1/2$ pence per ton-mile. The price of coal in Darlington fell from eighteen shillings (90p) to eight shillings and sixpence (42p) per ton.

A cargo of goods from New York could arrive in Liverpool in about 21 days though it sometimes took that length of time or longer to reach Manchester from there. A plan to link those places was carefully considered by Parliament in 1825 but already a storm of opposition to railways was being orchestrated by the owners of turnpikes or canals. When George Stephenson was called to give evidence about locomotives he was ridiculed, called a fool and branded a madman. He and his surveyors had frequently been assaulted as they tried to plan a route for the line. In spite of strong opposition in the House of Commons the Bill was finally passed in 1826 and George Stephenson was appointed principal engineer to the Liverpool & Manchester Railway Company at a salary of £1,000 per annum.

As the new line neared completion a decision had to be taken as to whether trains would be hauled by locomotives or by ropes attached to stationary winding engines. A prize of £500 was offered for the best locomotive to perform within the rules of the contest. Three engines were entered for the Rainhill Trials, namely the *Novelty* by Messrs. Braithwaite and Ericson, *Sans Pareil* by Timothy Hackworth, and *Rocket* by George and Robert Stephenson. *Rocket* was the outright winner, even reaching the undreamed of speed of 30 mph with seventeen tons behind the tender. Its superiority was partly due to the use of a tubular boiler containing 25 copper tubes surrounded by water through which the heated air passed on its way to the chimney. By this arrangement, in which a much larger surface area was brought into contact with the heat from the fire, much more steam was generated. This significant concept was incorporated into most steam engines thereafter.

This line – England's first inter-city route – was officially opened with great pomp and ceremony on 15 September 1830. The six locomotives, *Northumbrian, Phoenix, Rocket, Comet, Dart* and *Arrow* were driven by young engineers of the period. The following day *Northumbrian* drew a train with 130 passengers from Liverpool to Manchester in 1 hour 50 minutes. In 1831 an engine appropriately called *Samson* hauled a load of 164 tons over the same route in $2^1/2$ hours. This would normally have needed 70 horses.

Thus was born George Stephenson's dream of a vast network of railways throughout the country. In due course he received many accolades for his achievements but he never forgot the planners, architects, builders and engineers who supported him, nor the vast armies of navvies and labourers who made it all possible.

To the Honorable Philip Sydney Pierrepont

Hon'ble Sir

The Inhabitants of Brackley and the neighbourhood in their Exultation at the good Fortune which will confer upon them the Advantages derivable from the Rail-way to be extended from Bletchley to Buckingham and Brackley and which must speedily result in its connection with a Line to Birmingham cannot forget your strenuous and increasing cooperation in promoting the measure nor do they fail to perceive that without your vigilant attention the present Line might have terminated short of this Town.

The Inhabitants therefore beg you to accept their thanks not an ordinary expression of feeling but a sincere and grateful acknowledgement of Services which must be of great and may be of infinite importance to this Town and neighbourhood.

July 1846
A letter of thanks to the Hon. P S Pierrepoint. (Northamptonshire Record Office)

London & Sunderland
Royal Mail Coach.

FARES

TO BE PAID BY PASSENGERS TRAVELLING FROM
STOCKTON.

	MILES.	INSIDE.			OUTSIDE.		
		£.	s.	d.	£.	s.	d.
To Yarm - - - - - - -	4	0	2	0	0	1	4
Tontine Inn - - - - -	12	0	6	0	0	4	0
Thirsk - - - - - -	23	0	11	6	0	7	8
Boroughbridge - - - -	34	0	17	0	0	11	4
Wetherby - - - - -	46	1	3	0	0	14	4
Aberford - - - - - -	54	1	7	0	0	16	4
Ferrybridge - - - - -	63	1	11	6	0	18	6
Doncaster - - - - -	78	1	19	0	1	2	6
Bawtry - - - - - -	87	2	3	0	1	4	3
Retford - - - - - -	96	2	6	0	1	6	0
Tuxford - - - - -	102	2			1	5	0
Newark - - - - -	117	2	15	0	1	11	6
Grantham - - - - -	131	3	1	0	1	15	0
Witham-Common - - - -	141	3	5	0	1	17	6
Stamford - - - - - -	152	3	10	0	2	0	6
Stilton - - - - - -	166	3	15	6	2	4	0
Alconbury-hill - - - -	173	3	18	6	2	6	0
Buckden - - - - - -	180	4	1	6	2	8	0
Biggleswade - - - - -	196	4	8	0	2	12	0
Baldock - - - - -	204	4	11	6	2	14	0
Hatfield - - - - -	221	4	14	6	2	16	6
London - - - - - -	240	4	14	6	2	16	6
Castle-Eden - - - - -	14	0	7	0	0	4	8
Sunderland - - - - -	27	0	13	6	0	9	0

Small Parcels to LONDON, 10*lb.* or under, 3*s.* 6*d.* each; heavier Goods, 4*d.* a Pound. Passengers' Luggage, above 14*lb.* 4*d.* a pound to LONDON, and in Proportion to other Parts of the Road.

For Time of the COACH leaving the above Towns, refer to the Time-Bills or Proprietors:—viz. Mr. *Fretwell,* BOROUGHBRIDGE; Mrs. *Cass,* THIRSK; Mr. *Lamport,* CLEVELAND TONTINE INN; Mr. *Peverall,* STOCKTON; Mr. *Kipling,* CASTLE-EDEN; and Mr. *Jowsey,* SUNDERLAND.

** Packets and Parcels from HARTLEPOOL, SEATON, REDCAR, STOCKTON, YARM, &c. &c. may be conveyed to LEEDS the next Morning at 25 Minutes past 4 o'Clock, HALIFAX at 25 Minutes past 8, and MANCHESTER at 25 Minutes past 1 in the Afternoon.—Coaches from THIRSK to YORK every Evening.

N. B. The COACH sets off from STOCKTON for SUNDERLAND every Morning at 8 o'Clock, and from STOCKTON for LONDON every Afternoon at Half-past 2 o'Clock. Parcels and Passengers can go with this Conveyance by BRAMHAM MOOR to LEEDS, &c. the Rout the Bags of Letters now go.

(Darlington Railway Centre and Museum)

YORK Four Days Stage=Coach.

Begins on Friday *the 12th day* of April, 1706.

A LL that are defirous to pafs from *London* to *York,* or from *York* to *London,* or any other Place on that Road: Let them Repair to the *Black Swan* in *Holbourn* in *London,* and to the *Black Swan* in *Coney ftreet* in *York.*

At both which places, they may be received in a Stage Coach every *Monday, Wednefday* and *Friday.* which peforms the whole journey in Four Days, (*if God permits,*) And fets forth at Five in the Morning.

And returns from *York* to *Stamford* in two days, and from *Stamford* by *Huntington* to *London* in two days more. And the like Stages on their return.

Allowing each Paffenger 14l. weight, and all above 3d. a Pound.

Performed By
: *Benjamin Kingman,*
Henry Harrifon,
Walter Bayne's.

Alfo this gives Notice that Newcastle Stage Coach, fets out from York, every Monday, and Friday, and from Newcastle every Monday and Friday.

London to York: 1706 . . . 4 days. 2001 . . . some trains less than 2 hours. (Darlington Railway Centre and Museum)

*A reminder of past days is number 3020 **Cornwall** built by the London
& North Western Railway. It is shown at an open day at Crewe.*

(K Morton)

*In 1979 huge crowds turned out for the 150th anniversary celebrations of
the Liverpool & Manchester Railway. Midland Railway 4-2-2 number 673
holds centre stage at Rainhill. This class was known as 'Spinners'.*

(K Morton)

The Highland Railway 4-6-0 number 103 was restored to work special trains in the 1960s before being exhibited in Glasgow Transport Museum.
(Author's collection)

A Class 26 Bo-Bo, 26030, at Kyle of Lochalsh. This locomotive is in rail blue livery and carries the small version of the 'double-arrow' emblem.
(K Morton)

Modernisation did not happen overnight. This is a station in transition in 1970. It has a modern signal box with powered level crossing gates and colour light signals, contrasting with a disused water tank and water column. Part of a semaphore signal can just be seen beyond the latter.

(J A Wells)

*The striking livery of Rail Express Systems (RES) is shown to good effect on this class 47 locomotive, **Respite**, with a postal train. (K. Morton)*

ScotRail's chosen livery is illustrated by 47713, seen here on a push-and-pull service between Edinburgh and Glasgow. (K Morton)

*Network South East painted its stock in patriotic red, white and blue, which could not fail to be noticed! 50035 **Ark Royal** is at Waterloo.*

(K. Morton)

The opening of the Channel Tunnel in 1994 brought direct rail links between London Waterloo and Paris or Brussels. Two 16-coach Eurostars are seen at Waterloo International in 1995. They are capable of travelling at 186mph. (J A Wells)

Several colour schemes can be seen on Tyne & Wear Metro trains but some of the units are used for eye-catching advertisements such as this recruiting campaign for special constables. There is no doubt this is an arresting livery! (J A Wells)

An Intercity 225 express hauled by a class 91 electric locomotive hugs the coastline as it heads through north Northumberland. (K Morton)

Open days at railway centres have always been popular as they give visitors the opportunity of having a good look round. Great interest is being shown in the sidings holding locomotives for scrap, at Crewe, in the early 1980s. (K Morton)

*Contrasting liveries – 91022 in GNER blue and 91021 **Royal Armouries** in Intercity colours, 1997. (J A Wells)*

Electric multiple units, Class 325, have replaced diesel hauled postal trains on several routes. This is a 12-vehicle train (3 units coupled together) being used for crew training on the east coast main line.

(J A Wells)

The flamboyant livery of Class 220 Virgin Voyagers cannot fail to be noticed. These units, which have a speed of 125mph, are transforming travel, particularly on Cross Country routes. (J A Wells)

Teal blue and tangerine are the distinctive colours of 43081, at London St Pancras. (J A Wells)

Another livery to appear since privatisation is DRS – Direct Rail Services – which bought a small fleet of surplus locomotives. These fulfil contract work for the company but are also hired to other train operators.

(K Morton)

Contractors use weed-killing trains which consist of coaches to store chemicals and spray the tracks, and tankers to carry water. 20903 **Alison** *is at the rear of this unit and sister engine* **Lorna** *at the front.*

(J A Wells)

An 0-6-0 diesel shunter 08886 is moving a 'Walrus' bogie ballast tipper and a ballast plough, code name 'Shark'. (K Morton)

Track laying trains, ballast cleaners, stone blowers, rail grinders and tampers play a vital part in keeping the track in good condition. Tampers can not only pack ballast beneath the track, they can move the lines and sleepers sideways, correct alignment and lift rails to the correct height before packing round the sleepers. These operations are computer controlled. (J A Wells)

Stone blowers force small stones into the ballast to fill any holes and keep the track in the right place. (J A Wells)

Some companies imported Class 59 locomotives from Canada to haul coal or aggregates. 59202 pauses at Doncaster in July 1996. Later, National Power locomotives and wagons were transferred to EWS.

(J A Wells)

Formerly a shunter at the Clyde Valley Electrical Power Company's Clyde's Mill power station, O-4-0T number 3 is seen on passenger duty on the Bo'ness & Kinneil Railway. (K Morton)'

Cumbria and Repulse on the Lakeside & Haverthwaite Railway. These austerity 0-6-0 saddle tanks, built by the Hunslet company, were at the forefront of many industrial centres at one time, but others worked on British Rail. (K Morton)

Romney Hythe & Dymchurch Railway number 6 Samson about to leave Hythe. The powerful engines on this 13³/4 mile public railway can haul 14 full coaches. (J A Wells)

Robert Fairlie's ingenious locomotive was introduced in 1870 on the Ffestiniog Railway, the headquarters of which are still at Porthmadog in north Wales. (K Morton)

The only railway on a Scottish island is on Mull where a 10$\frac{1}{4}$ inch gauge line runs between the harbour and Torosay Castle, 1$\frac{1}{4}$ miles away. There are three steam locomotives but this view is of a diesel on the turntable at Craignure station. (J A Wells)

*The engaging Llanberis Lake Railway runs alongside the lake for two miles, giving wonderful views of Snowdonia, but also passing former slate quarries. The locomotive is **Dolbadarn**. (J A Wells)*

A Beyer Garratt 2-6-2+2-6-2 arriving at Dinas with a train from Caernarfon to Waunfawr on the Welsh Highland Railway. These locomotives were built in England for service in South Africa. No. 138 is one of those which has returned. (J A Wells)

A scene on the Tanfield Railway, County Durham, with an NCB 0-6-0 saddle tank hauling passengers in vintage coaches. (K Morton)

Chapter Two
STEAMING TO SUCCESS
(Early Days to Heydays)

In spite of opposition from politicians, scientists, farmers, journalists, doctors and various others who forecast doom, destruction and death, the construction of railways proceeded with haste throughout the kingdom requiring numerous bridges, embankments, tunnels and stations to be built.

The 1830s saw the development of lines spreading out from London to Bristol, Birmingham, Liverpool, Norwich and the south coast (as examples). Many of these railways were named after the places they linked. Ultimately there were numerous secondary routes too, and ribbons of shining steel revealed hundreds of branch lines throughout the British Isles.

The first cross-country line was authorised in 1829 and opened in stages between Newcastle on the east side and Carlisle on the west during 1835-38. With a length of 63 miles it was the longest stretch of main line to be sanctioned up to that time. The Newcastle & Carlisle Railway had only twelve first class carriages in 1839. These had glass window sashes, sprung seats, and were lined and stuffed throughout thereby giving more comfort to the eighteen passengers who shared the three compartments. Mixed (or composite) carriages had one first class and two second class compartments seating 22 in all, two less than a second class coach. The latter had open sides above the waist, which, as one journalist wrote "gave travellers an extensive view of the countryside".

An Act of 1844 promised third class passengers at least one train a day calling at all stations, in covered accommodation rather than seats in open coaches. Although the average journey at that time was fifteen miles, cheaper fares of a penny a mile encouraged people to travel further afield for the first time in their lives. Excursions to the seaside were always extremely popular.

In 1845 the number of railway projects for which plans had been lodged with the Board of Trade was 815 though some of these were fraudulent. This was the period of Railway Mania. George Hudson, a draper in York and later its Lord Mayor, supported various railway schemes by investing heavily in shares. He became chairman of several railway companies and aimed to establish rail links from York to London, Edinburgh and other important centres. People from all walks of life put their capital into railways but some lost heavily when their hopes collapsed. Other companies forged ahead and strengthened their positions by amalgamations and take-overs.

The name of Isambard Kingdom Brunel is synonymous with the original Great Western Railway whose main line ran from Paddington to Bristol. Although small of stature he was a strong-willed character and very determined. He chose a gauge of seven feet (after a while this became 7 feet $0^1/4$ inches) which gave much more space in coaches and wagons, a more comfortable ride and higher speeds. This was known as the broad gauge but it meant that passengers from other railway companies using the standard gauge had to change trains at junctions on the GWR system. Similarly, goods had to be transferred from one set of wagons to another. Bricks were a cargo that had to be handled individually – there were no pallets in those days! These difficulties were partly resolved by having certain tracks dual gauge, but subsequently the broad gauge was converted, the changeover taking several years.

Engineers produced numerous designs of locomotive, from the elegant to the downright ugly, each style according to the work it was to do, and painted in company colours with initials or the name of the railway in full on the tender. Many were named and some carried the company's crest. Smart, clean engines were always a good advertisement in themselves. In earlier days, as far as possible, each driver kept his own engine which was often treated with affection. One driver, giving evidence at an Enquiry, was asked what his reaction was when he realised his train was derailed. He replied, "I said 'Steady on old girl', put on the brake and hung on." Drivers were considered the elite, having progressed through the ranks of cleaner and fireman over several years. In the early 1880s some earned seven shillings and sixpence ($37^1/2$p) for each long working day, but this was considered good money. Spring buffers became standard fittings on Great Western engines during the 1850s and 1860s. They replaced the original leather stuffed with horse hair ones, which, according to the 'Guinness Book of Rail Facts & Feats', were sold off for use as music stools.

Early locomotives had brakes on the tender only, but these

were supplemented by brakesmen riding on the outside of carriages (until they were given more protection in brake vans) from where they applied the brakes when signalled by the engine to do so. Later, rail companies used either the Westinghouse air brake or the vacuum brake on their carriages which meant it was an advantage if some locomotives were fitted with both systems. In either case if the flexible pipes between coaches or locomotive were severed in a 'divided' train both parts had the brakes applied automatically. Under the Regulations of Railways Act of 1889 it became compulsory for trains in Great Britain to have automatic brakes fitted to all passenger trains so that they could be controlled from the locomotive. Even today that fact is ignored by film makers who seek to use a runaway train as their central theme.

From simple four-wheeled coaches there evolved six-wheeled vehicles then bogie coaches with four or six axles, all offering increased comfort. Prior to full sleeping car trains, a single first class sleeping car attached to a night express was introduced between Glasgow, Edinburgh and London in 1873. It travelled south one day and returned north the next. Within weeks the Great Northern Railway had provided stock to cover the other days. As the east coast route to Scotland was Great Northern territory to York, North Eastern from there to Berwick-upon-Tweed, and North British thereafter, jointly-owned coaches (East Coast Joint Stock – ECJS) were used for expresses from 1869. These all carried the GN varnished teak livery. Six years after the 'sleeper' the first dining car appeared. New corridor coaches of a superior design, including a restaurant car, were used on the 'Flying Scotsman' express from 1900.

Pullmans were first seen on the Midland Railway in 1874 and proved very popular, but it was the London Brighton and South Coast Railway which ran the first all-Pullman train a few years later. This train was electrically lit throughout, the power being generated by dynamos under the coaches and stored in batteries. It was also a Pullman train that was first fitted with buckeye couplings which acted also as buffers and, more importantly, helped to hold the coaches upright in the event of a derailment.

To give some idea of the number of passengers carried, in 1870 the railways handled 336 million; in 1880 it was 604 million and in the following year 623 million. These figures do not include the considerable number of journeys made by season ticket holders.

In spite of rivalry and competition, through coaches or complete trains passed daily over other companies' lines, linking towns and cities in different parts of the country. No less than seven railway companies used Carlisle at one time. For branch lines some railways used push-and-pull trains or steam railcars in an effort to reduce costs. On Tyneside the North Eastern Railway lost a lot of passengers to electric trams but the company's response was the introduction of fast, reliable electric trains in the Newcastle area in 1904, the first in the country. It is not surprising that the use of electric power became more widespread as it had some notable advantages like acceleration, braking, intensity of service and cleanliness.

As a means of providing better transport from the capital to the southern suburbs, London's first underground electric railway was the City & South London which ran from just north of London Bridge to Stockwell before it was widened and extended. This was followed ten years later, in 1900, by what was nicknamed 'the tuppenny tube', that is a uniform fare of two old pence, from Bank to Shepherd's Bush. These were the forerunners of the very complex system we have today. It was, however, the Metropolitan Railway which introduced the world's first underground passenger service, a dual-gauge route between Farringdon Street and Bishop's Road, in January 1863, before being extended to Moorgate almost three years later. Trains were steam hauled but the engines were fitted with condensing apparatus because of the tunnels. The carriages were lit by gas lamps.

After this flick through some pages of a railway album we can take a glimpse at the transportation of freight as the railways approached their peak of expansion. In 1881 the minerals conveyed by rail would fill a train stretching from London to York every day. A similar train for general merchandise would have been 86 miles long. These facts are from 'Our Iron Roads' by F S Williams (1883), a fascinating book which also records ". . . if we wish to form some estimate of the amount of our railway locomotion, we may look at the traffic of, for instance, the London & North Western Company, with its 1,766 miles of continuous railway, more than 10,000 miles in all, along which flows the trade of several of the chief towns and cities of the Empire;

carrying 50,000,000 passengers a year, or a million a week, equal in a month to the population of London; conveying 8,000,000 tons of general merchandise and nearly 26,000,000 tons of minerals; with 2,300 locomotives, 3,500 carriages and over 50,000 other vehicles that run a distance of more than 36,000,000 a year, equal to 1,458 times round the world; to say nothing of a magnificent fleet of steamships . . . its 40,000 servants . . . it is more like a kingdom than a company."

Farmers quickly found it paid them to send their milk to distant cities where it arrived fresh. A morning passenger train from Derby which left shortly after 8 a.m. would also convey eight to ten vans of milk, every one containing more than 40 churns, each of which held 16 gallons of milk – loose, not bottled – every day. Full train loads of fish and fresh meat were also sent to the capital.

At Camden Goods Depot, occupying about fourteen acres and with nearly twenty miles of sidings, 1,500 men were employed loading and unloading trucks, battling with bales, barrels and bundles, and parcels of every description weighing up to a hundredweight. About 670 wagons were loaded and despatched each night all over the country. An average of 25 trains arrived for unloading each night with all the bustle of having their loads sorted and transferred to carts for delivery. In spite of the fears expressed when railways were being introduced, more, not fewer, horses were needed in total and the traffic on canals was also increased.

In the early 1900s, as a common carrier, the railways were called upon to move a vast variety of loads – coal, foodstuffs, hay, cement, petrol, timber, glass, chemicals, furniture, machinery, steel products and livestock, to name a few. These were conveyed in open wagons, covered vans, or in specialised vehicles which included those used to transport long girders, transformers, milk, bananas, or military equipment. Most freight trains were loose coupled with three-link couplings but over a period of time more and more wagons were fitted with brakes which could be worked from the engine and were closer coupled.

It was an advantage when complete train loads could be worked through to their destinations as this saved the re-sorting of wagons at marshalling yards en route. By the early 1920s more than 100 individual railway companies were involved in the very complicated task of moving goods around the country and for export. Once the common use of trucks belonging to the various railways had been agreed, the Railway Clearing House, established in 1842, ensured that each company was properly paid for carrying others' goods, as was the case with passengers. In 1904 the RCH issued its first large 'Handbook of Stations' (which included junctions, sidings, collieries, works, etc.) in the United Kingdom. It showed whether there were facilities for handling passengers and parcels; furniture vans, portable engines and machines on wheels; livestock, horse boxes and prize cattle vans; and road carriages for conveyance by passenger train therefore needing an end-loading dock. The lifting capacity of any fixed crane was also given. There were subsequent editions but the original was reprinted in 1970, a very useful source of information.

When war was declared in 1914 the Government took control of the railways and appointed an executive committee of twelve top railway officials to take charge. Within a fortnight nearly 700 special trains carrying troops, food and military equipment arrived at Southampton, the port of embarkation, from all parts of the country. Numerous locomotives were commandeered for work in France. When large numbers of railwaymen joined the colours they were replaced where possible by women. The railways were called upon to carry more passengers and merchandise than ever before including millions of tons of coal to Royal Navy ships based in Scotland, normally taken by sea. Railway workshops also had to produce munitions. Maintenance of locomotives, rolling stock, track and equipment was reduced to a bare minimum. By the end of the war nearly half of the workforce had joined the forces. When hostilities ceased in 1918 the Government had a huge surplus of road vehicles which were then sold off. This had the effect of transferring traffic from rail to road; the railways lost their monopoly and things were never the same.

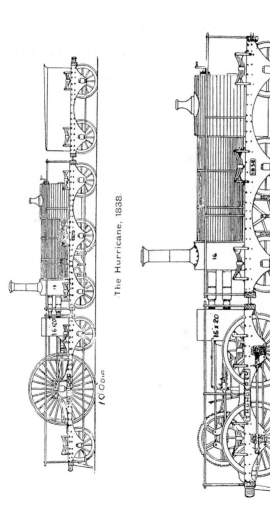

The Hurricane, 1838.

The Thunderer, 1838.

These unusual locomotives, built to Harrison's patent, were constructed by Messrs R & W Hawthorn of Newcastle upon Tyne for the Great Western Railway broad gauge. They had cylinders and motion on a separate carriage. The driving wheels of **Hurricane** *were 10 feet in diameter.*

(16³ $\frac{420.300}{29.7.56}$)

West Hartlepool Harbour and Railway.

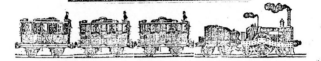

CHEAP TRIP

TO

BARNARD CASTLE.

On Tuesday, Aug. 5, 1856

A

SPECIAL TRAIN

Will leave WEST HARTLEPOOL, at 8 15, a.m. calling at the intermediate Stations up to NORTON JUNCTION inclusive, for BARNARD CASTLE, and return the same day, at 5 30, p.m.

FARES, THERE & BACK,

FIRST CLASS.   COVERED CARRIAGES.

3s. 6d.   2s.

Children under Twelve, Half-price.

No Luggage will be allowed.

An early application for Tickets will be necessary, as a limited number only will be issued.

SAMUEL CHESTER,

West Hartlepool, 29th July, 1856.   GENERAL MANAGER.

J. PROCTER, PRINTER, CHURCH STREET, WEST HARTLEPOOL.

(Darlington Railway Centre and Museum)

SOME DUTIES OF EARLY RAILWAY POLICE

Inspector of Police. 217. **Sub-Inspector of Police.**—Every Inspector or Sub-Inspector must issue to the Police in his district the proper Duty Papers, Notice of Extra Trains, &c.

218. He must take notice that no man is placed in charge of Switches, Signals, &c., who does not thoroughly understand the duties connected with them.

To superintend general conduct of men. 219. He must see that the men are clean in their persons, sober, and attentive to their duties; and that they are provided with the proper Lamps and Detonators; and have, and understand the Book of Instructions, and give a proper receipt for it in the book provided for that purpose.

Signals, &c. *Time bill of trains, &c.* 220. He must provide the Police at every post with a Time Bill of the Trains, and with a copy of any orders especially relating to that post.

To walk through district. 221. From time to time, at uncertain intervals, and both by day and night, he is required to walk through his district, and to report to his Superintendent, any irregularity which he may detect, either in the conduct of the men, or in the state of the Signals, Switches, &c.

Leave of absence. 222. Application from the Police for leave of absence must be made through him, and he will provide proper Supernumeraries in the event of leave being granted by the Superintendent.

Clothing. 223. The issue of Clothing to the Guards, Police, and Porters of his district is under his control; and he must take care that the proper exchanges are made, and that when a man leaves the service he delivers up his clothing, in accordance with the Regulations. (*See conditions of Service*).

Police, &c. to be acquainted with regulations. 224. **Police.**—All **Switchmen, Signalmen, Policemen,** and **Porters,** wherever employed, are to make themselves acquainted with the **"Conditions of Service," "Signals,"** and **"Precautions,"** and are to perform vigilantly and carefully all the duties which may be allotted to them; in every case where they **do not fully understand their duty, they must immediately** apply for instruction to the Superintendent, Station Master, or Sub-Inspector, **and no excuse of want of knowledge will be admitted** in the event of any irregularity or neglect on the part of Switchmen, Police, Porters, or others.

Duties of Police. 225. The duties of all **Policemen,** whether at Switches, Signals, Stations, or on the Line, are of a nature easily understood, but requiring great **care, attention,** and **watchfulness,** as the slightest neglect may lead to serious results.

Extracts from the rule book of the London, Chatham & Dover Railway Company, 1863. (National Railway Museum)

Advertising by the Great Eastern Railway. (National Railway Museum)

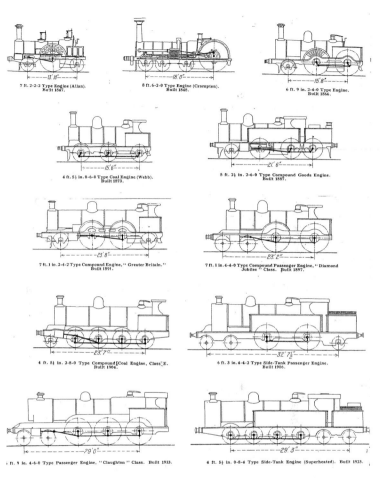

7 ft. 2-2-2 Type Engine (Allan).
Built 1847.

8 ft. 6-2-0 Type Engine (Crampton).
Built 1848.

6 ft. 9 in. 2-4-0 Type Engine.
Built 1866.

4 ft. 5½ in. 0-6-0 Type Coal Engine (Webb).
Built 1873.

5 ft. 2½ in. 2-6-0 Type Compound Goods Engine.
Built 1887.

7 ft. 1 in. 2-4-2 Type Compound Engine, " Greater Britain."
Built 1891.

7 ft. 1 in. 4-4-0 Type Compound Passenger Engine, " Diamond
Jubilee " Class. Built 1897.

4 ft. 5½ in. 2-8-0 Type Compound Coal Engine, Class E.
Built 1904.

6 ft. 3 in. 4-4-2 Type Side-Tank Passenger Engine.
Built 1906.

5 ft. 9 in. 4-6-0 Type Passenger Engine, " Claughton " Class. Built 1913.

4 ft. 5½ in. 0-8-4 Type Side-Tank Engine (Superheated). Built 1923.

A selection of locomotives built at Crewe, London & North Western
Railway. (Tenders, where appropriate, not included). Courtesy of the
'Railway Gazette'

Chapter Three
GROUPING – THE BIG FOUR
(1923-1947)

After being released eventually from Government control following World War I the railways were in a mess. Stopping short of full nationalisation, the Railway Act of 1921 decreed that all the railway companies – many of them formed by previous mergers – should be grouped into four, namely, in order of size, the London Midland & Scottish Railway, the London & North Eastern Railway, the Great Western Railway and the Southern Railway, their titles giving a very broad suggestion of their operating areas. Each was formed by uniting several major companies called the Constituents with a larger number of small organisations, the Subsidiaries. This scheme, referred to as the Grouping, was to be effective from 1st January 1923, therefore the period before that date became known as the pre-Grouping era.

CONSTITUENT RAILWAY COMPANIES

L M S
Caledonian
Furness
Glasgow & South Western
Highland
Lancashire & Yorkshire
London & North Western
Midland
North Staffordshire
(Number of Subsidiaries 27)

L N E R
Great Central
Great Eastern
Great North of Scotland
Great Northern
Hull & Barnsley
North British
North Eastern
(Number of Subsidiaries 26)

G W R
Alexandra (Newport & South Wales) Docks & Railways
Barry
Cambrian
Cardiff
Great Western
Rhymney
Taff Vale
(Number of subsidiaries 26)

S R
London Brighton & South Coast
London Chatham & Dover
London & South Western
South Eastern
South Eastern & Chatham Railway Companies' Management Committee
(Number of Subsidiaries 14)

The approximate route miles owned or jointly owned were:-
L M S 7,500; L N E R 6,700; G W R 3,800; S R 2,200.

NOTE : The 202 miles of the Northern Counties Committee in Northern Ireland, a 5ft. 3inch gauge line, together with a 3ft. gauge railway had been acquired by the Midland Railway and so became part of the LMS, to which was added the narrow gauge Ballycastle Railway in 1924.

Prior to 1923 each railway had had its own styles of locomotive and rolling stock, its own rule book, uniforms, methods of accounting, fare structures and management styles. Re-organising these companies and welding them together into formidable organisations, then introducing standardisation, was not something for the faint-hearted, but decisions had to be made and opposing ideas reconciled. The LNER alone took over no less than 236 different classes of locomotive. Although some excellent designs were included in the legacy presented to the Big Four not all others were successful.

*A procession of locomotives and rolling stock marked the Centenary of the Stockton & Darlington Railway in 1925. Number 25, **Derwent** was brought out of retirement for the occasion. (A E Ford Collection)*

A simple way of classifying steam engines is by the arrangement of their wheels, an American idea known as the Whyte system. Power from the cylinders is transmitted to the driving wheels which in the early days was a single pair but quickly progressed to four or six wheels linked together by coupling rods, and later to eight or ten. Ahead of these, at the front end, may be two or four smaller wheels (or none at all) and the same at the rear to spread the weight of the locomotive on the track. One with four leading wheels, six coupled (i.e. driving) wheels, and two at the back is a 4-6-2; one with only six coupled wheels is an 0-6-0. Tender wheels are not included. The variations are shown on the diagram below and some are illustrated by photographs elsewhere in the book. Where the engine has no tender to carry coal and water the letter T – for tank engine – is used after the number of trailing wheels, indicating the fuel is carried in a bunker and water in tanks on the loco itself, as in 2-6-2T.

0-4-0	2-4-0	4-2-2
0-4-2	2-4-2	4-4-0
0-4-4	2-6-0 (Mogul)	4-4-2 (Atlantic)
0-6-0	2-6-2 (Prairie)	4-4-4
0-6-2	2-6-4	4-6-0
0-6-4	2-8-0 (Consolidation)	4-6-2 (Pacific)
0-8-0	2-8-2 (Mikado)	4-6-4 (Baltic)
0-8-2	2-10-0	4-8-0
0-8-4		
0-10-0 (Decapod)		

Standard gauge Beyer-Garratt style in the UK were
2-8-8-2   or   2-6-6-2.

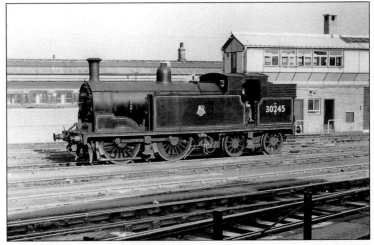

Class M7 0-4-4 tank engines were first introduced on the London & South Western Railway in 1897, then running on the Southern from 1923, and finally on the British Railways system. 30245 waits at Clapham Junction for its next duty in March 1957. (Ian S Carr)

*LNER B2 4-6-0s, introduced in 1945, were a Thompson rebuild of some Class B17s with 100A boilers and NE tenders. Renumbered by BR, **Blickling**, 61607, poses on Liverpool Street turntable in January 1957. (Ian S Carr)*

The four companies used other methods, too. The LNER favoured a letter to identify each class: A for all 4-6-2s, J for 0-6-0s, V for 2-6-2s . . . followed by a distinguishing number – B17, L1 etc. Broadly, the LMS had power for the criterion, ranging from 0 to 8 (the highest) for passenger, freight or mixed traffic, giving variations like 6P, 4F or 5P/5F, the latter shown later as 5MT. The Southern chose a letter and a number or simply a letter whereas the Great Western designated locomotives by giving each type a two digit class followed by two Xs to identify individual engines in the class – 47XX is one class, 4706 was one of them. This at least was the theory but there were variations. All four companies referred to some classes by a name which (as examples) included Schools and Merchant Navy shipping lines (SR), Kings and Castles (GWR), Patriots and Princesses (LMS), Antelope species and Football Clubs (LNER).

It was usual for the name of the Locomotive Superintendent who had led the design team to be shown ahead of the class – Wainwright class L, Gresley A3, Churchward 28XX. Large passenger engines on the LMS were normally painted red or green but various shades of green inherited from pre-Grouping railways predominated the liveries of the other three, although the

Gresley A4s looked particularly smart in garter blue livery and red wheels. The main colour for goods engines was black.

It is significant that the railways were privately funded whereas public money was used for road building. Road traffic was not subjected to the strict controls that were demanded of the rail industry.

To gain prestige and to attract the travelling public from other forms of transport the Big Four produced locomotives of incredible speed and power on their major routes. The first two Gresley Pacifics built by the Great Northern Railway at Doncaster in 1922 caused a sensation, then in 1923 C B Collett introduced his famous 'Castle' class, a most successful design. *Pendennis Castle* of the GWR and *Victor Wild*, an LNER engine, ran a series of trials on each other's tracks in 1925. As a result of these runs, Nigel Gresley (later Sir Nigel) modified his Pacifics and produced the world class A3s. The first authenticated locomotive to travel at 100mph was A3 number 2750 *Papyrus* but it was the Gresley streamlined A4s which really 'stole the show'.

No. 2509 *Silver Link* was only three weeks old when it hauled a special train from King's Cross to Grantham for rail officials and the press. It streaked along the main line on 27th September 1935, twice reaching 112 mph and ran for 43 consecutive miles at an <u>average</u> speed of 100 mph. Three days later this silver-liveried wonder inaugurated the 'Silver Jubilee' service from Newcastle to King's Cross in four hours, then ran the outward and return journeys each weekday for three weeks. A sister engine, No. 4468 *Mallard,* achieved a speed of 126 mph with the reserve 'Coronation' express set on 3rd July 1938, a world record for steam – verified by the dynamometer car — which will probably never be eclipsed. On the LMS, Royal Scot class 4-6-0 number 6113 *Cameronian* achieved a different world record by running 401.4 miles non-stop, beating the LNER's record of 393 miles (London – Edinburgh) set on 1st May 1928. Stanier Pacifics, some of which were streamlined, provided a very reliable source of motive power. GWR Kings and Castles were scheduled for spirited running, and we must not forget the sterling work of the Southern's King Arthurs, Lord Nelsons and the air-smoothed 4-6-2s. SR electrification also provided fast, intensive services. The first diesel electric locomotive for British main line use was No. 10000, introduced in December 1947 by the LMS, a foretaste of things to come.

During the 1930s the Public Relations departments of the railways broadened their publicity drives to encourage passengers to travel with their particular company. One aspect they focussed on was the greater use of named expresses. The oldest named train in the country – arguably in the world – was the 'Irish Mail', known unofficially as 'The Paddy', but there were the 'Flying Scotsman', the 'Golden Arrow', the 'Royal Scot', the 'Cornish Riviera Express' and many more which, to some, would probably sound superior to merely catching the 10.20! Railwaymen had their own local nicknames for expresses, like the 'Dog & Monkey', the 'Kiltie' and the 'Sprat & Winkle'.

Coach liveries varied even in each of the companies but most travellers recognised the varnished teak of the LNER, the maroon of the LMS, the chocolate and cream of the GWR and the green of the Southern. Each type of coach was given a distinguishing code for brevity. Two or three letters would indicate such vehicles as:-

FK   First class corridor (with gangway connections at each end)

CK   Composite corridor (more than one class)

RF   First class restaurant car

TO   Third class open coach (no compartments)

BTK   Brake third corridor.

In the previous section mention was made of faster goods services and this continued after the Grouping. They were known to many railwaymen as 'brakeys'. Nevertheless, a great number of goods trains continued to run using the standard three-link couplings, at about 25-30 mph. Provided they met coaching stock requirements, certain goods vehicles were permitted to travel on passenger trains when carrying urgent traffic. The conditions were that they were fitted with brakes worked from the engine, had a wheelbase of at least ten feet, screw couplings and suitable buffers. Horse boxes, cattle trucks, vans for perishable food such as fish, milk tankers and covered car transporters were in this category.

Each goods wagon carried its company initials — SR, LMS, GW, NE – its identification number, tare weight and carrying capacity. It may have had specific instructions such as NO LOOSE SHUNTING; To Work Between —— and ——; or when used for a particular traffic Return to Fletton (or wherever). Such wagons were

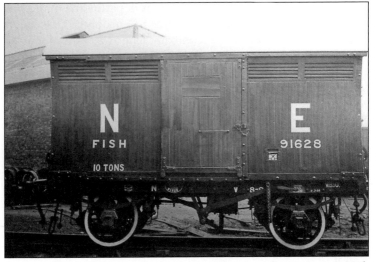

An example of markings on a goods van. These are: 1) Company initials – LNER or North Eastern; 2) Registered number; 3) Code name on plate or painted on; 4) Carrying capacity (10 tons); 5) Tare weight (8tons 9cwts); 6) Builder's plate.

This van also has on the solebars another plate to show carrying capacity; N for Northern Division; wheelbase 10 feet; date oiled, and V for vacuum brakes. It can be run on passenger trains because it fulfils the various requirements. (Darlington Railway Centre)

not in common use. Many trucks carried a code for easy identification:–

> Boplate   A long, bogied wagon for carrying steel plate
> Lowmac   A wagon with a low centre for machinery, etc
> Conflat   A flat truck for containers of various kinds
> Quad / Quint   Bolster wagons with four or five stanchions.

Each station or depot had to request daily the wagons it needed for loading. It was much simpler in those days to order, say, six Vanfits rather than 'six vans fitted with continuous brakes', or to request a number of Insixfish instead of insulated six-wheeled fish vans. The Great Western, always an 'individual' company, had its own distinctive codes such as Bloater, or Siphon G; even brake vans were Toads. Engineers' vehicles were named after aquatic creatures, so we had such names as Mackerel, Dogfish, Limpet, Walrus, Mermaid, Sea Lion and Shark. Generally speaking, unfitted wagons were grey, fitted ones red oxide, and insulated vans white. Privately owned wagons carried their own liveries.

Railway companies carried on other businesses than transporting passengers, animals and goods. They owned numerous ferries including train ferries to and from the continent; docks, harbours, hotels, refreshment rooms, cargo steamers, steamships on lakes, and canals; also some road and air transport. The largest customer was undoubtedly the Post Office. Every day thousands of bags of letters and parcels were carried in the guard's vans of passenger trains. The forerunner of this was an Act passed in 1838 which required railways to convey mails either by ordinary trains or special trains at such hours as the Postmaster General directed. The first Travelling Post Office was a converted horse box used on the Grand Junction Railway between Birmingham and Liverpool in 1838 although the Liverpool & Manchester Railway had been carrying mail from 1830. TPOs spread rapidly throughout the country, saving a lot of time by having letters sorted while the train was travelling. It was also an advantage to collect and deliver mail at speed. Pouches of letters were suspended from posts at the side of the track and were swept into a stout net on the side of a postal van as the train passed. The same van would drop off mail at these designated points. Postal staff at the lineside at night knew 'The Mail' was approaching when they saw two prominent white lights on the side of each Royal Mail coach in the train. At busy junctions some vans were transferred from one TPO train to another going to a different destination. Sorting vans and exchange apparatus were discontinued between September 1940 and October 1945. The last mail exchange was in 1971 at Penrith. [There are two preserved railways where the exchange apparatus can be demonstrated at slow speed.]

Moving on to the end of the 1930s, World War II was declared on 3rd September 1939 but preparations had been made beforehand. Once again the railways were taken under Government control. During 1940 and 1941 in particular they were prime targets for enemy bombers. One $2^{1/2}$ mile section near London was attacked nearly 100 times in nine months and suffered serious damage – but all over the country lines, junctions, marshalling yards, depots, bridges and viaducts were hit relentlessly. London and Coventry in particular were blitzed.

In his book 'The Railways of Britain', W H Boulton recorded how for one offensive alone 185,000 men, 20,000 vehicles and

220,000 tons of stores were carried to the ports of embarkation. This involved 440 troop trains, 680 special freights and 15,000 wagons by ordinary goods trains.

There was a huge increase in passengers, many of them service personnel. At times 20-coach trains were despatched from King's Cross with just one engine. Many British locomotives were taken away from vital work in our country to serve overseas including France and North Africa. Passenger coaches were converted into about 100 ambulance trains, many of which were sent overseas. Railway workshops, once they reached peak production of items required for use in the war, turned out more than half of the national total.

The above description can give only a thumb-nail sketch of what was achieved, rather like looking at one frame of a microfiche! There can be no question that without the railways victory would have been in doubt – yet they have never been given the recognition they deserve. The end of the war in 1945 left them in desperate need following a lack of normal maintenance. Nevertheless, pre-war liveries reappeared on locomotives, replacing the drab black of wartime. The LNER renumbered its whole loco fleet in 1946 and vast programmes of redevelopment were planned by all four companies, but it was not to be. The Government of the day refused to return them to their former owners and the Transport Act of 1947 put railways, collieries, canals and the London Underground under state control. They were nationalised from 1st January 1948.

THE SHUNTING POLE.

Never ride on a shunting pole.

This might be the result.

Before opening a carriage door from the inside, look out
to see if anyone is passing or standing outside.

DANGER ON TOP.

A fireman should not go on to the top of the tender
an engine in motion unless absolutely necessary, and th
only after having arrived at a definite understanding w:
the driver.

Be observant when working on the top of vehicl
especially in the proximity of over-bridges, signal gantri
or other such obstructions.

If the vehicle is in motion, the risk of injury is obviou

*Shortly after the grouping the GWR, LNER, LMS and SR issued a joint
booklet called "Prevention of Accidents to Staff Engaged in Railway
Operation". These are three examples.*

1825   1925

A   OF
CENTURY   PROGRESS

RAILWAY CENTENARY

PROCESSION
AND TABLEAUX

THURSDAY, 2nd JULY, 1925

A UNIQUE AND
HISTORIC OCCASION
WHICH CANNOT
RECUR

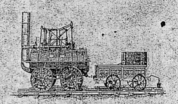

This is the cover of the brochure issued in 1925 to celebrate the centenary of the Stockton & Darlington Railway.

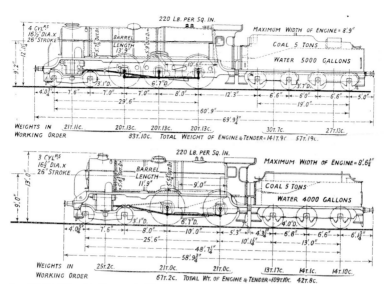

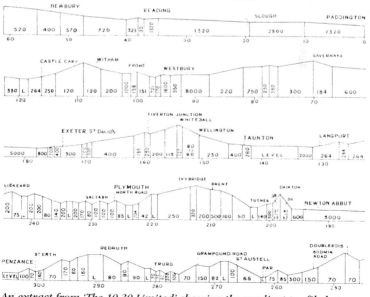

In 1946 The Railway Publishing Co issued a book called 'British Locomotive Types' compiled by the 'Railway Gazette' from official drawings supplied by the chief mechanical engineers of the four main line railways and the Ministry of Supply. These are two Southern Railway engines, a 'Lord Nelson' class and a 'Schools' class.

An extract from 'The 10.30 Limited' showing the gradient profile between Paddington and Penzance.

SPEED OF FREIGHT ROLLING STOCK.

General Rule **165**.

The following table shews the average speed at which L.N.E. stock may run under varying conditions :—

TYPE OF VEHICLES.	Average Speed m.p.h.		Distinguishing colour or loaded speed limit mark.	REMARKS.
	Loaded.	Empty.		
1. Open Goods and Sleeper Wagons .	35	35		
2. Open Goods*	—	—	Red.	
3. Plate, ordinary and trestle, load equally distributed up to full capacity . .	35	35		
4. ,, load unequally distributed.	25	—		
5. Salt, grease boxes . . .	25	25		
6. ,, oil boxes	35	35		
7. Bolster, load equally distributed up to full capacity . .	35	35		
8. ,, load unequally distributed or on more than three wagons . . .	25	—		
9. Machine, Flat, Boiler, Armour Plate, Economiser, load equally distributed up to full carrying capacity . .	35	35		
10. ,, load unequally distributed.	25	—		
11. Pulley, load equally distributed up to full carrying capacity.	35	35		
12. ,, load unequally distributed and exceeding 25% of carrying capacity .	20	—		
13. ,, load unequally distributed and not exceeding 25% of carrying capacity .	25	—		
14. Trolley, load equally distributed up to full carrying capacity.	35	35		
15. ,, load unequally distributed and exceeding 25% of carrying capacity .	20	—		
16. ,, load unequally distributed and not exceeding 25% of carrying capacity .	25	—		
17. Glass	35	35		
18. Cattle	35	35		
19. Cattle*	—	—	Red.	
20. Covered	35	35		
21. ,, *	—	—	Red.	
22. Gunpowder	35	35		
23. Meat, Perishable, Insulated* .	—	—	Red.	
24. Refrigerator*	—	—	White.	
25. Fish, open and covered* . .	—	.	Red.	
26. Bottom door wagons and Goods or Mineral Wagons used for Coal . . .	30	35		
27. Ballast Wagons	25	25	Blue.	
28. Tanks	25	35		
29. ,, (Starred) of not more than 20-tons capacity) . .	35	35		

Extract from 'LNER appendix to General Rules and Regulations and the Working Timetable, 1931'. This publication has 512 pages, plus index.

Chapter Four
THE BRITISH RAILWAYS PERIOD
1948-1994

Under the terms of the Transport Act of 1947 the railways of Great Britain, with a few minor exceptions, passed into the ownership of the British Transport Commission and were regulated by the Railway Executive. The railway system was split into six regions, namely Eastern, Midland, North Eastern, Scottish, Southern and Western though the Eastern and North Eastern were eventually reunited. Their boundaries followed the tracks of the Big Four but changes were introduced later to make them more geographical.

Over 20,000 locomotives passed into public ownership and from the outset a start was made to paint the words BRITISH RAILWAYS on tenders and tank sides. To overcome the difficulty of engines from the former companies having the same number, prefix letters E,M,S, or W were added. As coaches and wagons passed through the works company initials were obliterated and the same letters were placed before each vehicle's number. These letters also indicated which region was responsible for maintenance and repairs, SC being used for most of the Scottish region. Within two years, as part of a corporate identity, renumbering of locomotives was started as follows:-

Great Western retained their original numbers because they were on brass plates; Southern had 30,000 added to their existing numbers; LMS 40,000 or 50,000, and LNER 60,000. Standard locomotives, when they were introduced, were numbered in the 70,000s, 80,000s or 90,000s. Former wartime Ministry of Supply 2-8-0s and 2-10-0s were included in the latter.

A new logo of a very thin lion standing arched over a wheel and with 'British Railways' printed underneath its feet was introduced in 1950, quickly earning the nickname of the cycling lion, or the ferret and dartboard!

During 1948 fourteen classes of locos from pre-nationalisation companies were used for interchange trials in the different regions though some of their proven designs continued to be built before the standard types appeared.

After some deliberation the livery chosen for express engines was the GWR Brunswick green; the other principal colour was black, lined or unlined. A substantial metal number plate on the

Castle class 4-6-0 number 4097 **Kenilworth Castle** *brings an express from Swansea into Paddington on 14 June 1959. The white buffers suggest the locomotive has been on recent Royal Train duty. (Ian S Carr)*

smokebox door of all steam locomotives was introduced, following LMS practice. Classes used by the Big Four were retained but all engines were given a power class of from 0 to 8 (later 9), another LMS innovation. Lower down on the smokebox door was also a small, oval shed-plate giving a number and a letter. 'A' denoted a main or parent shed, B/C/D etc were subsidiary depots. For instance, at one time Nine Elms on the Southern Region was 70A – the principal depot having overall responsibility for 70B Feltham, 70C Guildford, 70D Basingstoke, 70E Reading, 70F Fratton, 70G Newport (Isle of Wight), 70H Ryde (Isle of Wight).

On the cab side of tender engines and in the bottom corner near the cab of tank engines was shown the letters 'RA' followed by a number 1 to 9 – the Route Availability. Each route, or wherever there were lines, was assessed for weight bearing particularly on bridges, overhang of vehicles on curves, gradients and clearances, so locomotives were restricted accordingly. An RA 1 engine could be used anywhere but an RA 5 had limitations and an RA 9 such as a Duchess had more.

The first British Railways standard locomotive, a power class 7 Pacific for mixed traffic (7MT) was introduced in 1951. It was number 70000 *Britannia,* forerunner of the Britannia class which carried names such as *William Shakespeare, Coeur de Lion* and *Earl Haig.* There followed another eleven classes, all designed under the supervision of Robert Riddles and showing a definite similarity to LMS styles. 4-6-2 number 71000 *Duke of Gloucester* (8P) was the only one of its class but it was preserved after withdrawal and made into a much more efficient machine. The last steam locomotive for BR was 2-10-0 number 92000 *Evening Star,* built at Swindon in 1960. It was finished in passenger livery, the only 9F to be painted green. [Perhaps it is significant that, many years before, another Great Western engine had been named *Morning Star.*] The performance of locomotives could be assessed at Derby Test Plant, a joint LMS/LNER project which was commissioned in 1948.

Significant changes were slow in coming but the re-introduction of the 'Flying Scotsman' express running non-stop between King's Cross and Edinburgh in May 1948 was a step in the right direction. The following year this non-stop service was re-allocated to a new express named the 'Capitals Limited' which ran ahead of the Scotsman. It was renamed 'The Elizabethan' in 1953 to mark the Coronation of Queen Elizabeth II and within months was covering the 393 miles in 6½ hours.

Work on electrification schemes, which had been held up because of the war, was resumed. The Liverpool Street to Shenfield suburban route was completed in 1949 and the Sheffield – Manchester line through the Pennines via the Woodhead tunnels introduced electric traction five years later.

The first British Railways mark I coaches appeared in 1951. They were constructed of welded steel which made them safer than wooden-bodied coaches in the event of an accident. The chosen colour was carmine and cream: at least that was the official name but some people preferred to call it 'plum and spilt milk' and others referred to it as 'blood and custard'! Pre-nationalisation stock was repainted over a period but it was not long before there was a change to maroon and the whole process started again. Parcels trains in particular presented a colourful array of vans from the four companies. In 1957 a new logo for locomotives was introduced which was also used on coach sides in a smaller, circular form.

Green diesel multiple units (dmu's) began to replace steam sets on secondary routes and branch lines from 1954. Some were assembled in railway workshops at Derby and Gloucester but many were supplied from other builders, notably Cravens and Metro Cammell.

With fewer people travelling, the Government had to consider how to win passengers back to rail so an optimistic Modernisation Programme was launched in 1955, which – if it had been fulfilled – would have cost up to an estimated £1.5 billion even though lines were already being closed. Hopes were raised when it was announced that steam engines were to be phased out in favour of a rapid switch to 100mph diesels and electric traction. In the mid 1950s there were only five diesel locomotives capable of working main line trains but faster services between major cities were planned over a fifteen year period, which of course would require better track and more advanced signalling. There would be many more marshalling yards to speed up freight services. Major electrification between Euston, Liverpool and Manchester would be only the initial stage of total electrification of the west coast main line. On the Southern region power from a third rail would be extended. The plan stated that freight services were to be remodelled and there would be a wide programme of refurbishment of stations and parcels depots.

Of the numerous diesel locomotive designs from several manufacturers many were unreliable or inadequate for their duties as they had not been sufficiently proved in operation before large orders were placed. In the early days the locomotive's number was preceded by the letter 'D' (for diesel) but subsequently each class was shown by the first two digits of the number, like 31— or 47—. Before this was introduced diesels could also be partly categorised by power class, 1 to 5 at first, or by their wheel arrangement. For shunters the 0-4-0 or 0-6-0 of the Whyte system was still used but the remainder depended on whether the axles were powered or there simply to spread the weight of the locomotive. Those with only two, powered, axles in each bogie were referred to as BO-BOs whereas three powered axles at each end were CO-COs. As a variation there were also some CO-BOs built. Carrying axles were shown by the figure 1 giving A1A-A1A (two driven axles with a carrying pair of wheels between) and 1CO-CO1. To give extra braking assistance on slow, heavy freight trains a brake tender was coupled to the locomotive but this was not necessary once all wagons were fitted with air brakes.

One of the most successful diesel designs was the English Electric CO-CO 'Deltic', a fast powerhouse of 3,300hp. The prototype, now in York Museum, was introduced in 1955, followed by 22 production models in 1961-62, distinctive in two shades of green. Later, these were class 55. They took over expresses from Gresley Pacifics on the east coast main line.

Meanwhile, the introduction of Blue Pullman trains on the Midland and Western region's lines in 1959 had brought what promised to be a new era for business travellers. Unfortunately, support from other passengers continued to decline and in the early 1960s the Government engaged Dr Richard Beeching from industry with a brief to review the railways – not, it should be noted, transport as a whole. After a mere five years the new vision of Modernisation was given a severe knock when huge sums of public money were poured into the system of motorways to the detriment of the railways. It did not end there.

Dr Beeching did identify wasteful practices like having rakes of coaches standing idle in sidings for long periods, local trains with hardly any passengers, and goods trains with only a few wagons. His first report, 'The Reshaping of British Railways', precipitated drastic action and devastating consequences. 250 rail services were withdrawn, and more than 2,000 stations and goods yards were closed. About 5,000 route miles of railway were shut down and a lot of the track lifted for scrap. Huge gaps were left in parts of the rail network to be eagerly filled by nature, farming or building. Some of the recommendations made sense but – with the benefit of hindsight – was saving money at the expense of future needs the right option?

In the years leading to the final withdrawal of the iron horse the majority of steam locomotives were filthy and often badly maintained. Work-stained engines were sent out from their depots to haul even important expresses and charters. A notable exception was number 46238 *City of Carlisle* which was turned out immaculately from Carlisle Upperby whenever it hauled trains of football supporters to away matches. Railway enthusiasts flocked to ride on special trains with particular engines, believing that after August 11th 1968 steam would be gone for ever. These trains ran all over the country, in fact some engines that were to be used were specially cleaned by volunteers.

BR's last standard-gauge steam train on its way from Liverpool to Carlisle pauses at Rainhill with Class 5 4-6-0 45110. 11 August 1968. (Ian S Carr)

On August 3rd there were unprecedented scenes at Liverpool as hordes of railway enthusiasts sang 'Auld Lang Syne'. They sang "God Save our Gracious Steam": they chanted a thunderous "STEAM! STEAM! STEAM!" – but let the magazine 'Railway World' of August 1968 continue the story:-

> "They gave three cheers for Steam, three cheers for the crew, three boos for diesel, and under the splendid direction of someone wearing a top hat and cloak, they sang 'John Brown's Body Lies A-mouldring in the Grave But STEAM Goes Marching On' . . . The passengers from the train joined in – old people, young people, on the cab, off the cab. The whistle worked again and the hundreds replied, the songs started again . . . and for one hour and under the benevolent eye of one policeman and his dog, Liverpool Exchange was turned into a cathedral of contempt for diesel, and into a flashing, singing, wine-dripping, thronging last celebration of Steam's lost cause."

On the last day, what became known as the Fifteen Guinea Special ran from Liverpool to Carlisle. Black Five No. 45110 hauled the train to Manchester where Britannia class No. 70013 *Oliver Cromwell* took over for the run on the Settle & Carlisle line. On the return trip 44871 and 44781 gave a lively performance. Meanwhile, last trains running on branches that were to be closed were packed.

When the official list of locomotive types to be preserved was issued in 1961 there was no A3 included. Many people were horrified and it prompted Mr Alan Pegler to buy *Flying Scotsman* from British Railways in January 1963. This is without doubt the world's most famous locomotive. He was given a contract for the engine to haul charter trains all over the country. After the steam ban, which excluded Scotsman, it was 1971 before BR relented and allowed *King George V,* then owned by Bulmer's Cider, and hauling that company's Pullmans, to go on a one-off tour, but more did follow . . . and steam specials were resurrected!

Moving ahead to the second half of the BR era, the British Transport Commission was abandoned in favour of the British Railways Board in 1963. Another deliberation brought a further change of corporate logo which appeared in 1965. Out went the distinctive lion holding a wheel in its forepaws and in came modern thinking in the form of two arrows pointing in opposite directions. Was this suggesting an electric flash of inspiration, or were the cynics nearer the mark by daring to imply that BR did not know which way it was going? When diesel locomotives were painted blue and had this white symbol enlarged on each side of the body it did nothing to enhance their appearance. It was about then that the title British Railways was dropped in favour of the more up-market (?) British Rail. A further change of locomotive livery to grey seemed to reflect the depressed state of the railways. Nevertheless, in spite of the cutbacks by various Governments, some progress was made. In 1971 mark II coaches appeared, followed by mark III in 1973. These were high speed diesel trains which proved very successful after their introduction between Paddington and the west country. On a later test run one unit achieved a speed of 143 mph; another completed a non-stop run between King's Cross and Edinburgh in five hours. After improvements to track and signalling these trains were timed to run at 125 mph, giving them the name of Intercity 125s. Power cars at each end have a 2,250 horse power engine giving a total output of 4,500hp.

Electrification of the west coast main line in the early 1960s brought faster travel between Euston and Glasgow but it was June 1991 before mark IV coaches hauled by class 91 electric locomotives, or driven from a driving van trailer (DVT) in the other direction, gave similar benefits to the east coast route. These trains were known as 225s because of their ability to run at 225 *kilometres* per hour. Experiments with tilting trains were abandoned when funding was withdrawn, leaving the field open to competitors from abroad.

As road traffic into city centres increased, local councils were faced with the dilemma of reducing the number of cars and buses clogging the streets but at the same time making it easier to reach main shopping areas, bearing in mind that main stations were often some distance away. The first scheme in the country to tackle this problem was the Tyne & Wear Metro which had its nucleus at Newcastle upon Tyne. The initial section opened in 1980. Interchange centres were built where cars could be parked in the suburbs. The people from them, and bus passengers, would then transfer to the rapid rail system. Some routes were taken over from British Rail and modified but other sections were specially built. These included five underground stations serving different parts of the city, one of which was below Newcastle Central. Following the deregulation of buses the idea of reducing their numbers in the main thoroughfares had to be abandoned. Manchester, which was the second Metro scheme, chose modern trams running through the streets on

A scene to gladden the heart of any colliery manager! The yard at Ashington, Northumberland, is full of merry-go-round and colliery wagons in August 1985. The diesel shunter is NCB number 7; the BR locomotive is 56076 **Blyth Power.** *(Ian S Carr)*

rails at road level and using platforms at the main railway station. In parts of London the Docklands Light Railway provides an innovation by having driverless trains.

On the freight side there was a gradual, if somewhat slow, change to have all wagons air braked from the locomotive and concentrating more and more on running block trains through to their destinations, thereby cutting out re-sorting at marshalling yards en route. Furthermore, wooden bodied wagons were replaced by steel vehicles with larger capacity. As a comparison there were 1,400,000 goods wagons running in 1946, 850,000 in 1963 and 13,379 in 1975. Once brakes were fitted to all goods stock there was no need for a brake van at the rear of each train, just a tail lamp on the last vehicle.

With the introduction of computers, which quickly became very sophisticated, each style of wagon was given a three-letter computer code in addition to its registered number. This applied also to infrastructure vehicles but these retained their aquatic creature names.

Following cutbacks in freight facilities an attempt was made to continue some wagon load trains under the name of Speedlink, using modern rolling stock. This was quite a successful enterprise but when it was no longer cost effective the service was withdrawn in 1991.

British Rail introduced sectorisation in 1987 with freight divided into four main sectors – petroleum products, metals, construction material such as aggregates and cement, and coal. For the latter new wagons were built and kept in rakes, usually of 36, for working between a colliery and a power station or port, thus giving them the name of 'merry-go-rounds', or MGRs for short. This system superseded all the shunting and sorting in colliery yards. Railfreight or Railfreight Distribution attended to traffic which was not included in the other categories. Much greater use was made of containers that could be transferred easily from road to rail for express conveyance before being put back on the road for final delivery. Later, with an eye to future privatisation, freight was split into three zones in the mid nineties, namely Load Haul, Mainline and Transrail.

What must be ranked as the engineering achievement of the 20th century, the Channel Tunnel, was opened for rail traffic in 1994, a truly historic occasion. The first regular lorry shuttle

When British Rail introduced sectorisation in 1987 each freight sector had its own decal. 56091 is a representative of the coal sector – hence the black diamonds. (K. Morton)

through the tunnel began on 19th May, followed a month later by the first Railfreight train. Three months later was the first car shuttle though this service was not fully operational until the end of the year. Eurostar passenger trains were introduced in the November and can whisk passengers through northern France to Paris or Brussels at speeds up to 186mph. Long freight trains linking places in the UK with various countries in Europe give a wonderful variety of goods wagons to the railway observer.

Modernisation meant the closure of hundreds of signal boxes throughout the country as the absolute block system became obsolete on main lines. By that method of controlling trains a line was assumed to be blocked until it was proved to be clear. Now computer controlled electronic devices indicate a line is clear unless it is shown on the illuminated track diagram to be occupied. The entire route between King's Cross and Edinburgh is controlled by just nine signalling centres but in the year 2000 there were more than 600 mechanical signal boxes still in use in mainland Britain.

British Rail ceased from 1st April 1994 in favour of a return to Privatisation. Many scenes from the BR period are recreated on our preserved railways – but with clean, well-cared for locomotives and stock.

At one time it was planned to run Eurostar trains from Glasgow, Edinburgh and Newcastle to the continent, but this idea was dropped. Before that decision was taken a complete set was hauled to Glasgow by two class 37s for clearance trials. It is entering the Down loop at Morpeth before heading north. (K. Morton)

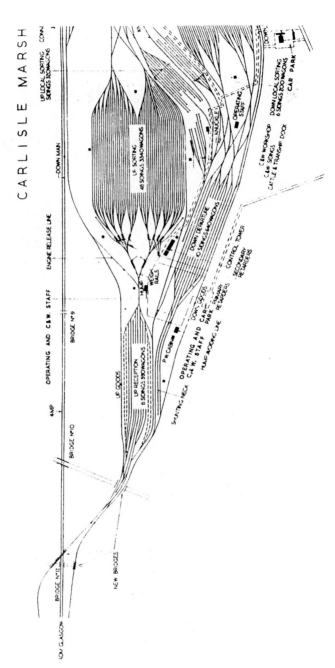

Carlisle marshalling yard, circa 1960. (Author's collection)

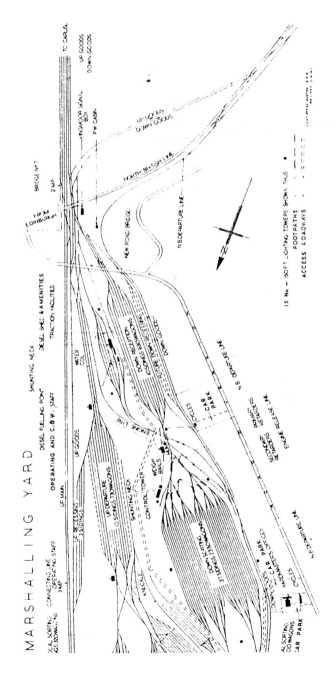

Carlisle marshalling yard, circa 1960. (Author's collection)

RAILWAY TRAFFIC RECEIPTS
4 weeks ended 22 April 1956 compared with 1955

	1956 £000's	1955 £000's
Passenger Train Traffic	13,078	12,572
Merchandise, Minerals and Livestock	11,809	11,976
Coal and Coke	9,248	8,809
TOTALS	£34,135	£33,357

16 weeks ended 22 April 1956 compared with 1955

	1956 £000's	1955 £000's
Passengers	32,226	31,004
Parcels, etc. by Passenger Train	13,513	12,310
Merchandise and Livestock	32,443	33,726
Minerals	16,119	14,989
Coal and Coke	39,362	37,110
TOTALS	£133,663	£129,139

Railway Traffic Receipts

4 weeks ended 9 September 1962 compared with 1961

	1962 £000's	1961 £000's
Passenger Train Traffic	19,010	18,610
Merchandise (inc. Livestock) and Minerals, etc.	9,180	9,980
Coal and coke ..	6,820	7,330
Totals	35,010	35,920

36 weeks ended 9 September 1962 compared with 1961

	1962 £000,s	1961 £000's
Passengers	114,760	111,970
Parcels, etc. by Coaching Train	39,470	38,600
Merchandise (inc. Livestock)..	65,190	69,500
Minerals, etc. ..	25,620	30,630
Coal and coke ..	69,690	71,100
Totals	314,730	321,800

Chapter Five
PRIVATISATION
(New Opportunities for our Railways)

In April 1994, following the Railways Bill of the previous year, there was a complete reorganisation of the railway system as a prelude to Privatisation. Briefly, the chosen path to denationalisation was that the track, signalling, control centres and stations would be owned by Railtrack, not retained by Government as first thought. Infrastructure Services would be responsible for the maintenance and renewal of track and infrastructure; Train Operating Companies (TOCs) would run the trains using locomotives and rolling stock hired from leasing companies to be known as ROSCos. It was the intention to dispose of every part of railway business from the handling of parcels to research, repairs, testing and maintenance. In all about a hundred separate aspects were sold off over a period.

Railtrack, which was floated on the stock market in May 1996, retained only fourteen major stations and charged for their use. The remainder – about 2,500 in all – were leased to the various train operators. The Government had invited applications from companies that were interested in running train services over specified routes or areas. Each bid was considered on its merits by the Office of Passenger Rail Franchising, taking into consideration frequency of service, updating or renewal of trains, fare structures, how much it would cost (or save) the Government – that sort of thing. In all 25 franchises were agreed for terms ranging from seven to ten or even fifteen years. The first two, awarded in 1996, were given to South West Trains (owned by the Stagecoach bus company) working out of London Waterloo and, after some initial problems, to Great Western Trains. This was a management buyout, later sold to another bus company, First Group, whose trains then ran as First Great Western to and from London Paddington. What was seen as 'the jewel in the crown', the east coast main line, was handed over to Sea Containers Limited and trades under the name of Great North Eastern Railway. There are historical connections here linking to the Great Northern, North Eastern and the Great North of Scotland Railways! The west coast route was won by Richard Branson who was also awarded the challenge of Cross Country Services. He uses the names Virgin Trains and Virgin XC. The last of the 25 was sold to Merseyside Transport Limited (MTL) who changed the name of Regional Railways North East to Northern Spirit. Subsidies were given to each company, reducing year on year, after which the operators were expected to pay premiums to the Government. All the Train Operating Companies have to pay Railtrack for each train run. The Office of the Rail Regulator, with a staff of well over 2,000, and, later, the Strategic Rail Authority still left the Government with considerable power.

TRAIN OPERATING COMPANIES IN THE YEAR 2000
Anglia Railways
C2C Rail (formerly London Tilbury & Southend Rail)
Cardiff Railway
Central Trains
Chiltern Railways
Connex South Central
Connex South Eastern
First Great Eastern
First Great Western
First North Western
Gatwick Express
Great North Eastern Railway
Island Line (Isle of Wight)
Merseyrail Electrics
Midland Mainline
Northern Spirit
ScotRail
Silverlink
South West Trains
Thames Trains
Thameslink
Virgin CrossCountry
Virgin West Coast
Wales & West
West Anglia Great Northern

A massive response by the TOCs has seen huge investments in new rolling stock, highly colourful and eye catching in their distinctive liveries. In the year 2000 Railtrack itself spent £2$\frac{1}{2}$ billion and the train operators together with ROSCOs placed orders worth the same amount. Within three years passenger traffic had increased by some 30 per cent.

It was thought at first that the three freight companies – Mainline, Load Haul and Transrail – would be sold off individually to generate competition, but all three were bought by an American company, Wisconsin Central, in 1996. At first it was proposed to trade under the name North & South Railways but this was quickly changed to the more embracing English Welsh & Scottish Railways – EW & S, but soon to be simply EWS. The distinctive bright red and gold livery with prominent number and initials immediately commanded attention. 250 new diesel locomotives, class 66, were ordered from General Motors and built in Canada to replace many ageing and prone-to-failure BR locos. The company's crest shows the superimposed heads of a lion, a dragon and a red deer stag.

In the last years of British Rail parcels and mail were handled by Rail Express Systems, known as RES. This became part of the expanding EWS, as did Railfreight Distribution. Goods yards, sidings and depots throughout the system were leased from Railtrack. EWS was determined to increase its share of traffic, aiming to triple the amount carried within ten years. Its policies of extending wagon load trains – the Enterprise Service – and of meeting customers' requirements, in contrast to the 'cannot do' of BR, has won praise for initiative but the Government's agreement to allow 44-ton lorries on the roads may prove to be another handicap for the railways. New wagons in maroon livery are in service and additional orders were placed by EWS for fleets of high capacity, high speed vehicles. A total of 2,500 (February '01) included 845 bogie coal wagons each carrying 75 tonnes and having a tare weight of 102 tonnes. The first of these were handed over from Thrall Europa of York early in 2001. Nineteen of these vehicles are the normal train load.

Freightliner has also expanded its operations and is proving to be a strong competitor for EWS. Now known as Freightliners Limited, the company not only conveys containers between ports and customers' centres, and international traffic through the Channel Tunnel, but also engages in infrastructure and contract work which includes heavy haulage of coal, and cement. It has its own fleet of class 66 locomotives which are hired to other operators when needed, subject to availability.

To speed up Royal Mail deliveries new Railnet sorting centres were opened by the GPO in various parts of the country, connected by diesel or electric hauled mail trains, or dedicated class

325 electric units. These run in units of four vehicles but two sets are often combined to give greater capacity. With more passenger trains being run to cope with demand, an increase in freight, accommodating charters, and frequent freight trains from Europe there is just not the capacity to offer all the additional 'paths' train operators would like. At the beginning of the new millennium urgent discussions were under way to ease congestion by exploring the possibilities of re-opening closed routes, upgrading existing but under-used lines or laying completely new high speed tracks. Meanwhile, if train operators cause delays, say because of a train failure, they have to compensate Railtrack at up to £160 per minute: similarly Railtrack has to pay the same rates to TOCs when they are prevented from running to time because of track or signalling faults. Added to this was the 'big stick' wielded by Government for the railways to reach impossible targets. Hooligans causing vandalism, trespassers, suicides, and lorries or buses hitting bridges are just a few examples of what can delay trains.

A broken rail which caused the Hatfield crash on 17th October 2000 resulted in additional stringent checks being made to all 19,800 track miles. Initially 850 emergency speed restrictions of 20 mph, or in some cases as low as 5 mph were imposed by Railtrack though some were lifted after a few days. Then, at the end of October, nature unleashed violent storms across the country which devastated widespread areas by flooding and caused unprecedented disruption. Hundreds of fully grown trees, warehouse roofs, garden sheds and portable buildings, even caravans, were strewn across railway lines. There were major landslips, some more than a mile long; many tons of ballast were washed away leaving track suspended at crazy angles, and overhead power lines were brought down. The result was total chaos on the railways (and on the roads) as services were cancelled. Shortly afterwards there was additional trouble when more storms hit the country. Towards the end of the year it was heavy snow and freezing fog which added to the misery. Thousands of passengers abandoned the railways when emergency timetables, which changed often, showed the frequency of trains halved and journey times doubled, or worse. No one can recall such upheaval nationally, even in wartime.

It was six months before things began to get back to normal. Over the years railways have suffered from unfair competition, severe war damage, and strikes which penalised the very people who supported them, but they battled through. However, the events towards the end of the year 2000 had a profound effect. The cost to Railtrack for renewals and compensation was phenomenal and seriously affected on-going investment, which put the plans of train operators in jeopardy.

After a horrendous year it seemed that Railtrack was beginning to 'surface' but the nightmare was not over. In October 2001 the Government announced with no prior warning that Railtrack PLC was to be the subject of a Railway Administration Order and no further financial support would be given, hence trading in shares was suspended.

Putting Railtrack into Administration was very costly for the Government. The company given responsibility for managing its affairs was Ernst & Young, and this continued until October 2002 when a new non profit making organisation, Network Rail, replaced Railtrack. This was considered by many people to be 'part re-nationalisation by the back door'!

Chapter Six
INDUSTRIAL RAILWAYS

Impressive locomotives hauling fast expresses and, by contrast, goods engines slogging up gradients with long freight trains would be for many a general impression of railways in the fifties and early sixties, but beyond these, in the background, were hundreds of tank engines, mainly 0-4-0s and 0-6-0s, shunting wagons around sites all over the country. These unsung heroes were the workhorses at innumerable industrial centres.

NCB 0-6-0 saddle tank hauling railway-owned 21-ton coal hopper wagons to exchange sidings, 1973. This engine has been saved by the Tanfield Railway. (J A Wells)

The oldest industry served by railways was coal mining where in colliery yards and sidings, covering 250 or more acres, empty wagons brought in by railway locomotives were dragged away by 'tankies' for loading, and full trucks were shuffled into train loads ready for despatch to industry or for domestic use and export. Coal companies bought some of their engines new but often snapped up redundant stock from the four main railways. Many of these were from pre-Grouping days. Some were tender engines which were particularly useful for handling heavier trains between collieries in a group and for taking train loads of coal to shipping points some miles away. This may have necessi-tated running on railway tracks for part of the way, thanks to special agreements made years before. As designs of coal wagon evolved and capacities increased, collieries were happy to buy the older, surplus vehicles from railway companies for internal use. Even chaldron waggons were still in use in the Durham coalfield for a long time. Old track was also given an extended life and it was possible to find rail 'chairs' showing dates of manufacture in the 1880s, more than 80 years later.

Chemical production in 1960 accounted for over 9% of British manufacturing output and remains a major industry. Its diversity includes fertilisers, dyes, explosives, soaps and detergents, plastics and pharmaceuticals. Vital raw materials are provided for dozens of other industries. In the 1950s much of the rail traffic used to be carried in special hopper wagons with gravity discharge for powdered substances, but Presflo wagons used compressed air to unload their contents. A variety of tank wagons carried liquids in bulk, some of them highly dangerous. At the end of the decade about 7,000 tanker wagons were owned by chemical and allied companies. Small containers of different types were widely used for powdered or granular loads. The works shunters at such complexes were thus an essential part of the organisation but alternative forms of propulsion – diesel or fireless locomotives – had to be used in certain situations.

Heavy industries could have 40-50 miles of track, including sidings. As an example, ingots, blooms, slabs, bars, rolled strip, railway wheels and tyres, and various forgings were manufactured at one steel works in Yorkshire. Train loads of light scrap metal were pressed into bundles, then transferred to furnaces in the melting shop. There were five access points to the array of BR sorting sidings and the main line, via which 4,000 tons of oil arrived each week, along with 600 tons of dolomite and large amounts of coal. 400,000 tons of 'unfinished' or 'semi-finished' goods were despatched in one year. Transferring this traffic to and from the works and moving steel from one process to another required careful co-ordination of the locomotive fleet.

Shipbuilding also relied heavily on the railways to supply the raw materials but this industry found it very beneficial to use some locomotives fitted with a crane above the cab for lifting and moving smaller parts.

Major ports used to depend on the railways to bring in goods for export and similarly to distribute a huge variety of imports throughout the country. Before the days of the Channel Tunnel and containerisation, train ferries carried wagons that met international standards to and from the continent. They were marked with an anchor. There were tracks in profusion serving wharves, docks and warehouses but during World War II, when military traffic added enormous burdens to an already stretched system, it was necessary to supplement British locomotives with United States 0-6-0 tank engines. Their design was not to everyone's liking but there is no doubt they performed with gusto!

Principal suppliers of industrial locomotives for many years were Bagnall's, Andrew Barclay, Beyer Peacock, Hudswell Clark, Cockerill & Co., Hunslet of Leeds, Kerr Stuart, Peckett's of Bristol, Robert Stephenson, and Manning Wardle.

So what happened to all these industrial locomotives? Obviously many were scrapped but we are fortunate that so many have survived and continue to give much pleasure on heritage railways. They include some of the American shunters and the British built Austerity 0-6-0 saddle tanks, but overall there is a good, interesting variety. It is worth recording also that coaches, wagons, signals, track and equipment have been donated to various groups, railway centres and museums by firms anxious to play their part in railway preservation.

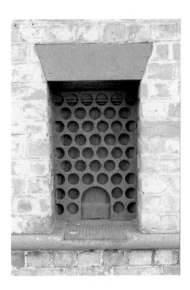

Chapter Seven
NARROW GAUGE RAILWAYS

In the early days of railways, when the system was just being developed, it was the custom to use a narrow gauge railway to remove spoil or to carry material to the construction site. Such a line was referred to as the 'temporary way' because it would be removed once the 'permanent way' was in place. Even today track workers are known as p-way men. Narrow gauge railways were used similarly in the construction of reservoirs and dams, or for the extraction of timber.

In collieries, underground railway systems were well developed, being used for many years for pit ponies to haul tubs of coal from the coal face to the shaft from where they were raised to the surface. The coal was washed and sorted into grades before being loaded into standard gauge trucks. In a similar way the output from a quarry was often taken to a railhead for loading.

At many mills, refineries, factories, shipyards, steelworks, potteries and brickworks (et alia) narrow gauge lines were laid around the site along with standard gauge tracks. Elsewhere whole railway systems were installed which were cheaper, occupied less ground, could go where larger gauges could not, and did not need the strength of infrastructure. In Wales slate quarries in particular made full use of such lines. As they were all privately owned and seldom connected with others the actual gauge was a matter of choice. Let us look first of all at three railways which have been in use for many years but still provide the service for which they were designed.

The 15-inch gauge Romney, Hythe & Dymchurch Railway was officially opened as a tourist attraction in July 1926 between Hythe and New Romney in Kent, a distance of eight miles. Not only was it very popular with visitors, it was used for public transport in the area. The locos could pull loads of 60 tons. Over the next two years the line was gradually extended by $5^{1}/_{2}$ miles to Dungeness, south of Romney. During World War II the coastal area where the RH&DR runs was declared a prohibited zone and the railway was used for military purposes. The little railway became known for carrying all the equipment and parts for a pipeline which would be laid under water to France, to supply petrol for our land forces. A notable feature during the war was an armoured train that patrolled the line and was said to have shot down an enemy aircraft. Most locomotives, which are built to one-third size, are based on the design of LNER Pacifics, others were Canadian style 4-8-2s. After the war it took two years to reinstate the line and stock which had survived on a bare minimum of maintenance; thereafter visitors returned in droves. It continues to be a very popular passenger-carrying railway with the superb engines from the 1920s and 1930s still giving sterling service. At a Gala in the spring of 2001 the railway created a new record by having nine locomotives hauling 32 coaches from New Romney to Dungeness. Railway Squadron soldiers are trained to take over railways damaged in war and make them serviceable for transporting supplies and refugees. Annual camps for Territorial Army units use various railway groups for training purposes so it is not surprising that the RH&DR has been included in this scheme, to mutual benefit.

Snowdon, the highest mountain in Wales, has five peaks, the main one of which, at 3,560 feet above sea level can be reached by travelling on the Snowdon Mountain Railway from Llanberis. It was built during the early 1890s to a gauge of 2 feet 7^1/$_2$ inches and opened in 1896. Because of the steep incline, with a gradient of 1 in 5^1/$_2$ in some parts, the railway is unique in Great Britain in that it works on the rack and pinion principle developed in Switzerland. Each train comprises a locomotive and one coach which seats 60 people and is pushed to the top. There are three intermediate stations where trains can pass on the 4^3/$_4$-mile journey that takes an hour in each direction. The seven locomotives are all Swiss built and the coaches are bogie vehicles with glazed windows. On a clear day the views are spectacular but if it is dull or cloudy it can be dismal!

Owners of a quarry in the mountains at Blaenau Ffestiniog in Wales had great difficulty transporting slate to the harbour at what is now Porthmadog until a 1 foot 11^1/$_2$ gauge line, the Ffestiniog Railway, was authorised by Act of Parliament in 1832. Horses were used at first to pull empty trucks back to the quarry but when the trucks were loaded they ran down by gravity with the horse deftly stepping into a dandy cart (a low, flat truck) at the back of the train and being carried along. In 1864 the Board of Trade gave permission for passenger trains to run, the first time narrow gauge railways were used for this purpose.

From that time trains were steam hauled. It was on this railway that a novel design was introduced in 1870. The engineer, Robert Fairlie, developed an ingenious idea of having two engines joined back to back as one articulated unit, running on a powered bogie at each end – an inspiration that caused interest worldwide. These locomotives were used on heavier trains and were very versatile machines as they removed the need for double heading and always faced the right way! The reduction in demand for slate by the 1920s, together with the withdrawal of passenger trains at the beginning of World War II, caused the total closure of the line in 1946 when almost everything was abandoned *in situ.* Then a preservation society saved the line and the first trains were running again in 1955. Thereafter various extensions gave a length of over thirteen miles.

Some other narrow gauge lines can give an idea of the tremendous variety that can be found. Another 15-inch gauge tourist line is the Ravenglass & Eskdale Railway, which runs for its entire length of seven miles in the stunning scenery of the Lake District National Park. Originally it was a 3ft. gauge railway opened in 1875 to carry raw materials to ironworks at Barrow-in-Furness and Workington but when passengers were first carried some months later the demand exceeded the seating capacity. The poor state of the track forced the withdrawal of services in 1908. The line was closed some years later and the track removed. Part of the bed was used when a new company re-laid track to the smaller gauge in 1915 to transport granite. This traffic helped to supplement the income from passenger services, which had been reinstated, but these were withdrawn again because of the war and not reintroduced until the fighting in Europe had ended. When the railway was put up for sale in 1958, after changes of ownership, it was purchased by the Ravenglass & Eskdale Railway Preservation Society, and after a great deal of hard work became a very popular tourist attraction. *River Irt* is said to be the oldest 15-inch gauge loco in the world still working.

The Isle of Man Steam Railway runs for $15\frac{1}{2}$ miles from Douglas, the capital, to Port Erin. This is the remaining part of a network which was originally 46 miles long, built to a width of three feet in the 1870s as part of the island's transport system and as a tourist attraction. Traffic declined in the 1950s but now thousands of visitors a year, many of them railway enthusiasts, enjoy this link with the past. Thirteen of the original sixteen locomotives supplied by Messrs. Beyer Peacock or Dübs, still provide the motive power, and some of the carriages are also from the 19th century, though they have been modernised.

In Scotland the only island railway is on the Isle of Mull where it has the further unique distinction of being purpose built to connect a stately home at Torosay with the harbour at Craignure, which has a regular ferry service to the mainland. It is open to the public and the $10^{1}/_{4}$-inch gauge, $1^{1}/_{4}$ mile run embraces views of sea, mountains and woodland. There are three steam locomotives and two diesels.

Some narrow gauge lines have been laid on sections of the track bed of disused standard railways. When hopes of acquiring the Alston branch in Cumbria failed, the South Tynedale Railway developed the alternative. The Kirklees Light Railway, near Huddersfield in Yorkshire, and the Bure Valley Railway at Wroxham in Norfolk are two further examples, the latter being constructed on part of the East Norfolk Railway, later the Great Eastern.

Driverless trains for Post Office use on the London Underground commenced operations in 1927, after work had started in 1914. Built to a gauge of two feet, this $6^{1}/_{2}$-mile line ran between Eastern District Post Office and Paddington. In the mid 1970s it was carrying 30,000 mailbags a day; today fifty trains run at two-minute intervals, eighteen hours a day, six days a week. They carry an estimated four million letters on any single day, which to move by road would take 100 seventeen ton lorries.

On narrow gauge railways some locomotives and stock are of very unusual designs but there is no doubt there is a timeless charm and character about them and they have served us well for many years.

PART TWO
SOURCES OF INFORMATION
(AND INSPIRATION)

The first part of this book gave a very condensed history of the railways of Great Britain to provide a basic background in advance of further studies. We now look at sources of information to expand your knowledge of railways, but it is necessary to compromise and point the reader in the right direction by using only a selection of examples relating particularly to libraries, record offices, heritage railways and museums.

Chapter Eight
LIBRARIES

Northumberland County Library has branches throughout the county which are co-ordinated from their headquarters in Morpeth. Being largely a rural area, mobile library vans make regular visits to the more remote places. The Dewey system of classifying books is used by Northumberland as in most libraries. It is an international arrangement devised in 1873, based on ten main groups of subject matter each of which contains 100 numbers and decimal sub-divisions. Railways are listed under 385. Some of the sub-divisions are stations 385.314, bridges and viaducts 385.312, signals 385.316, timetables 385.2042, freight wagons 385.264, and uniforms 385.092.

For issuing books Northumberland has recently adopted a computer recording method. If a specific book is not held in stock every effort is made to obtain it on loan from elsewhere. Beyond the bookshelves is a reserve store of books and other publications particularly for subjects of local interest, but special permission to look at these is granted to bona fide readers for reference or research purposes. Similarly, arrangements can be made to consult work deposited with the library by individuals following submissions for degrees, or from private investigations.

Press cuttings relating to the local area were meticulously filed but this service was affected by financial cutbacks in recent years. Photographs are no longer handled by the library, having been transferred to the County Record Office; but relevant maps in different scales are held, including 6-inch first editions. Northumberland's libraries do maintain records of clubs and organisations and are pleased to display posters announcing their activities, though exhibitions of any kind are charged for. Various magazines are available each month and can be read on site, or in many cases borrowed. Computer time can be booked in order to access the Internet. Other aspects of the service which do not apply to railways are omitted from this survey but Northumberland County Library does pride itself on having very helpful and knowledgeable staff.

The Central Library in Cardiff has a large collection of books relating to railways as part of the Transport Section. Books about railways in the vicinity of Cardiff are held in the Local Studies

Department which also houses a collection of theses and dissertations, maps, news cuttings and local newspapers. Railway photographs form part of the main local collection. Much of the 'old' stock is stacked away but is readily available. Books not held in stock can normally be obtained via the Regional Library Service. Aberdeen is included as the representative of a university library. Members of the public are welcome to visit the Special Libraries & Archives but books have to be ordered in advance and are brought in at 09-30, 12-30 and 14-30. Most manuscript and archival material can be made available very quickly, though it is advisable to check.

Their library cataloguing system is Dynix, an American method. Aberdeen holds a large assortment of transport material in the O'Dell Collection, which was bequeathed by a former Professor of Geography. It includes about 200 items associated with the Great North of Scotland Railway. Photocopying, scanning copies of older material, and photographic work is undertaken by staff members but many items held in the university are too fragile or valuable to copy. All reproductive services are bound by current copyright legislation. The department has two self-service microfilm/microfiche reader-printers.

Oxfordshire Central library in Oxford is the hub of the county's Cultural Services. Books for loan are processed by using the computerised issue system on a reader's membership card. Books in the reference section can be consulted by anyone, and those that are in store will be produced when asked for. Details of various organisations are on file but can also be accessed on the County Council's website. Maps and newspapers are available for reference.

Over 300,000 photographs are held in the Photographic Archive at the Centre for Oxfordshire Studies, which has the advantage of being in the same building as the library. The collection, which continues to expand, includes road and rail transport. It is possible to order copies of most photos but some are held for reference purposes only. Oxfordshire is digitising its collections with the aim of putting on-line images into local libraries and museums, and making photographs available on the web. Other facilities in the Centre include computer terminals, a display area, and microfilm or microfiche readers.

The Irish & Local Studies library of the Southern Education & Library Board in Armagh, Northern Ireland, holds a substantial collection of books on Irish railways but these are for reference only on the premises. Included are maps, newspapers in bound volumes and microformat, postcards, and some photographs.

Newton Abbot library keeps an extensive collections of books and publications covering all aspects of standard, broad, and narrow gauge railways.

We are indeed fortunate in that such wide-ranging facilities are available in warm, comfortable surroundings.

(See also Railway Societies)

In his book 'Whishaw's Railways of Great Britain & Ireland' (1842), Francis Whishaw, an engineer, gave many details of early railways. The following is an extract relating to The North Union Railway in Lancashire.

DETAILED COST OF THE RAILWAY – The following abstract of the quantities and cost of the works upon the line of the North Union Railway, twenty-five miles in length, with the general heads of expenditure in the various departments, is the first document of the kind we have met with; and we trust the example set by Mr. Vignoles will shortly be followed by the engineers of all other lines in the kingdom:–

Earthwork . .	2,903,028 cubic yards (average 10¾d. per yard)		£ 125,676 3 11		
Masonry and Bridges	100,265 cubic yards masonry £113,096 0 5				
	325 tons iron-work	3,875 0 0	120,248 15 1		
	25,022 cubic feet timber	3,277 14 8			
Fencing and Drains	87,712 lineal yards.—*N.B. This includes road-diversions, &c., gates, &c. &c.*		20,533 2 7	£394,826 19 4	
Upper Works	6,885 tons of iron rails and chairs . .£66,833 17 7				
	91,545 lineal yards of railway, laid on blocks and sleepers, including ballast, drains, walling, bolts, keys, felt, plugs, and small materials and labour	61,538 0 2	128,368 17 9		
Land and Damages	320 acres for railway			49,342 3 10	
Stations . . .	Land for stations £17,257 15 5				
	Station-buildings	13,589 8 1	£44,278 0 0		
	Warehouses	9,266 0 0		88,960 4 5	
	Fixtures, turn-plates, and sundries . . .	4,164 16 6			
Carrying Establishment	Repairing-shops, tools, and fixtures . . .	11,884 0 0			
	Locomotive engines, tenders, &c. . . .	18,863 6 7	43,682 4 5		
	Carriages, horse-boxes, trucks, &c. . . .	12,934 17 10			
Interest	Interest-account, rates, taxes, &c. &c		4,746 15 8		
Management .	Parliamentary and law-expenses	17,147 8 0			
	Engineering and surveying	6,193 5 9	42,055 12 11	46,802 8 7	
	Office-expenses, travelling, advertising, &c.	3,134 19 2			
	Salaries	15,580 0 0			
Total Cost .	. . . .			£ 578,931 16 2	

Thus the average cost per mile is 23,157*l.* 5*s.* 6*d.*, a sum comparatively small when set in juxtaposition with the actual cost of several other main lines of railway.

The receipts and disbursements up to the 30th June, 1840, were as follows :—

Receipts.

Coaching-department	. £28,861 17 1
Coal-department	. 467 16 5
Merchandise-department	. 2,564 10 5
Rental account	. 500 0 0
	£ 32,394 3 11
Profit and loss account, to 31st December, 1839 . . .	. 406 11 5
	£ 32,800 15 4

Expenses.

Coach-disbursement account	.£ 1,982 14 5
Locomotive-power account	. 3,783 1 9
Office-expenses account	. 207 13 11
Salary-account	. 853 2 0
Toll (to Liverpool and Manchester Co.) account	. 7,189 17 2
Petty-disbursement account	. 12 13 10
Interest-account	. 140 19 0
Interest on loan-account	. 766 11 10
Tax and rate account	. 502 0 4
Chief rents account	. 43 13 4
Charge for direction account	. 300 0 0
Maintenance of way	. 600 0 0
Compensation	. 3 3 0
Fire-insurance	. 2 12 6
Advertising	. 2 9 0
Repairs for buildings	. 13 9 11

	16,404 12 0
	£ 16,396 3 4

Dividend of 50*s.* per share on 6329 shares is 15,822*l.* 10*s.*

Thus the disbursements in carrying on the traffic of this railway for six months, ending 30th June, 1840, amounted to 16,404*l.* 12*s.* ; being equal to 51·43*l.* per cent on the coaching, coal, and merchandise revenue.

The expenditure in the locomotive-department was at the rate of 7,546*l.* 3*s.* 6*d.* per annum ; the cost of maintenance of way was at the rate of 1200*l.* per annum, which is equal to 48*l.* per mile. This is, indeed, a very small sum as compared with the expenditure in this department on other lines.

Chapter Nine
RECORD OFFICES

Record Offices are fascinating places which are visited by thousands of people researching a multitude of different interests. Of those related to railways long lists could be compiled from original papers which include local chronicles, also collections from businesses, estates, organisations and from private individuals or families. Archives consist of hand-written documents on paper or parchment, printed records, maps, plans, drawings and photographs. Record Offices accept responsibility for the permanent preservation of items given to them, or deposited on long loan, and make them available for research. (It is always advisable to book an appointment before visiting any county repository.) Each Record Office is unique because of its particular treasures: again we shall look at a small sample to show their individuality.

Cornwall

Documents at Cornwall Record Office in Truro are listed in different ways – calendared, catalogued, box-listed, or bundle-listed. The only collection which relates specifically to railways contains the deposited plans for proposed railway schemes in the county, although there are large amounts of records in the categories mentioned above relating to the Redruth & Chasewater Railway Company, for example. Parish and subject indexes are available on open shelves which can be used to access collections, including railways. These should lead the enquirer to the catalogues, then the documents.

Cornwall's Record Office does not keep collections of local newspapers but these are available on microfilm at the Cornish Studies Library in Redruth. Photographs can be perused by members of the public and copies ordered if required. Photocopies can be requested from any documents suitable for copying but not if they are likely to be damaged in the process. A postal search and copying service is available and free information leaflets can be supplied. (A large stamped and addressed envelope is always appreciated.)

Hertfordshire

At the Archives & Local Studies Centre for Hertfordshire, in County Hall, Hertford, an automated archive cataloguing system is being introduced. As new material is acquired an 'interim list' or detailed box-list is created which is then catalogued in a word processing format, and a paper copy is made available in the public reading room.

Several railway companies had routes through Hertfordshire. The first railway to be built was the London & Birmingham, opened in 1837, which was incorporated into the London & North Western Railway (later the LMS). Main lines of the Midland Railway, the Great Northern and the Great Eastern railways also ran for some distance through the county. About 750 documents – mainly maps, plans, records relating to the requisition of land, copies of Railway Acts (also proposed schemes which never materialised), books of reference, reports, and accounts – form a major collection covering the period 1836-1938. It also includes some 60 branch lines before they were amalgamated with larger companies. Similar documents are held relating to the Metropolitan Railway from 1845 to 1946, and various light railways.

There are additional miscellaneous references to railways in other collections, which are detailed on 28 subject cards under that title. They include prospectuses, timetables, reports and correspondence from the 19th and 20th centuries. Researchers are helped by a names index, places index, subject index, and several relating to maps. A broad selection of local newspapers and journals is held in the library. Items of interest, including railways, are indexed. These are kept available in hard copy for six months; after that, articles are put onto microfilm for which a reader-printer can be booked. Press cuttings from publications not normally taken but which would enhance the collections are also kept. Hertfordshire County Council sets out rules for people requiring photocopies or copies of photographs. Researchers will be given any help they need, but for those who know the references of the material they wish to consult, a phone call in advance of the visit will ensure it will be ready for them when they arrive.

Liverpool

At Liverpool a CALM 2000 system has recently been acquired for cataloguing documents and to conform to the professional standards established for use by archivists, although members of the public in the search room continue to use paper-based finding aids with a manual index at present.

Some material relevant to the Liverpool Overhead Railway is available and papers of J W Williams, the contractor, from 1887 to 1893. Naturally, their archives contain diverse references to the Liverpool & Manchester Railway and its subsequent owners, including letters and papers from George Stephenson. There are also documents from the Chester & Birkenhead Railway, and some British Rail Property Board files. Visitors must have a valid reader's ticket to gain access to the search room where they can use request slips to order up to five items at a time. These are delivered every half hour.

Maps, photographs and cuttings relating to railways can be consulted in the same way as other material. Liverpool Record Office does not offer a reprographic service for photographs at present but readers can take their own copies, and make photocopies of documents. A colour laser copier is available. A publication, "Transport on Merseyside – A Guide to Archive Sources" can be consulted or bought in the library, or copies can be bought by post.

Northamptonshire
Northamptonshire CRO has a substantial amount of material relating to railways, a large proportion of which consists of deposited plans dating from 1830 (the original London & Birmingham Railway line) to 1937 (LNER: Charwelton). These plans embrace large companies like the London & North Western Railway, the Great Northern and the Great Eastern, and numerous smaller railways – or proposals – of which the following are examples:-

Buckinghamshire & Northamptonshire Railway
East & West Junction Railway
Lancashire Yorkshire and Great Eastern Junction Railway
Midland Counties & South Wales Railway
Peterborough Sutton & Wisbech Railway.

Northamptonshire has used card indexes for personal names, subjects, maps and pictorial references, together with catalogues for main collections, but a computerised archival cataloguing system (SEAX) has been introduced. Railway documents are very varied and encompass track layouts, pay slips, sales of land, a vicar's life and work among navvies, books of reference, letters, petitions and staff books.

Northamptonshire Record Office

Scottish Record Office

Following the Transport Act of 1968, archives of the British Railways Board appertaining to English and Welsh railways were transferred to Kew, but those relating to Scotland are now preserved in the Scottish Record Office at Edinburgh. This collection comprises records and printed material which includes a specialised library of books and periodicals relating to the Caledonian, Glasgow & South Western, Highland, Great North of Scotland and the North British railways – the Scottish Big Five – and to the Scottish areas of the LNER and the LMS. Added to these archives are private collections which have been deposited, covering, with other subjects, engineering, technical drawings and Mutual Improvement Classes.

Most research, but not all, is done by authors and enthusiasts concentrating on timetables, particular lines; and stations, features, or rolling stock worth modelling.

The Scottish Record Office has a series of leaflets, one of which is "Facilities for Historical Research".

Public Record Office

Finally, a glimpse at the Public Record Office, Kew, near Richmond in Surrey. It is the national archive for the United Kingdom, the Nation's Memory, whose holdings fill virtually *100 miles of shelving and cover 1,000 years of history* from the

Domesday Book to the latest Government papers released to the public. Hundreds of people use the reading rooms every day but on the PRO's website people from all over the world can search through the catalogue of over eight million items!

At one time railway companies retained many of their own records and it was possible to make enquiries for information from their Public Relations & Publicity Officer. Economic measures, reorganisations and clear-outs meant that accumulations of papers deemed to be out of date and no longer relevant were thrown out, their historic value being overlooked or ignored. Nevertheless, other pieces were sent to the PRO in their thousands.

Documents are catalogued by a unique in-house system called 'PROCAT' but access to the collections is by a variety of means. There is a "computerised catalogue, which is also available online, as well as paper catalogues and different finding aids." All documents and records have a special reference. They can be ordered in advance or on the day of the visit to the PRO and are brought to the reading rooms usually within half-an-hour. Readers are loaned a pager on registering for each visit and are allocated a particular table space. The pager tells you when your order is ready.

The Public Record Office Image Library can supply prints or transparencies of any item in any document, subject to the usual safeguards, which will be photographed to order if not already on file. Photocopying of documents can be ordered on site or by post through the Record Copying Department. Estimates will be given for a maximum of five records per estimate, incurring a minimum charge of £10 sterling (June 2001). Should your request amount to more than £10, including handling and despatch, details of the balance required will be forwarded to you. If you ask for an estimate but do not subsequently place an order the £10 charge is not returnable.

The majority of documents at the PRO are Crown Copyright which means they can be reproduced free of charge in any format or medium provided it is done accurately and not used in a misleading context. The source of the material must be identified and the copyright status acknowledged. State of the art digital scanning equipment can produce paper copies of records in various sizes, or they can supply images in a range of electronic formats. Traditional photocopying methods are being phased out for preservation reasons.

You will have noticed that specific collections have not been identified – there are just too many of them! If this section sounds intimidating help is always at hand, and after your first visit things are always easier. It is worth bearing in mind that if you are unable to visit Kew in person you can engage the services of an independent researcher. A list of such people can be obtained from the Readers' Information Services department.

Finally, anyone who visits a Record Office must remind himself or herself that these documents are irreplaceable and must therefore be treated with great care and respect, otherwise they will not be available for future generations to enjoy.

IMPERIAL TABLES & METRIC EQUIVALENTS

MONEY 12 pence (d.)	= 1 shilling
20 shillings (s. or sh.)	= 1 pound (£)
WEIGHT 16 ounces (oz.)	= 1 pound (lb.)
14 lbs.	= 1 stone (st.)
** 2 st.	= 1 quarter (qr.)
** 4 qrs.	= 1 hundredweight (cwt.)
20 cwts.	= 1 ton

(** usually omitted in favour of 112 lbs., or 8 st., = 1 cwt.)

LENGTH 12 inches (ins.)	= 1 foot (ft.)
3 feet	= 1 yard (yd.)
22 yds.	= 1 chain (ch.)
** 10 ch.	= 1 furlong (furl.)
** 8 furl.	= 1 mile

(** usually omitted in favour of 1,760 yds. = 1 mile)

1 shilling = 5p

£1 = 100p

1lb = 0.4536 kilograms or kilos

1 cwt. = 50.802 kg

1 ton = 1.016 kg

1 inch = 25.4 millimetres (mm)

1 ft. = 0.3048 metres (m)

1 yd. = 0.9144 metres

1 mile = 1.6093 kilometres (km)

Chapter Ten
MUSEUMS & RAILWAY CENTRES

Museums are one of the most prolific sources of information about railways where everything can be seen in three-dimension, full size and assembled in a convenient viewing area. Each has its own individuality.

A general museum in most provincial towns and cities will include sections of data and various exhibits relating to local railways, depending on how much space is available. Some places concentrate on the theme of transport and show railways as part of the whole whereas others relate more to industrial or engineering themes. At Derby, a town that grew up round the railway industry, emphasis is on locomotives, rolling stock and signalling systems which have been built there. Eastleigh, another railway centre, includes the re-creation of part of the locomotive erecting shop together with the typical home of an engine driver.

Museums can feature a particular area rather one specific place. At Conwy Valley Railway Museum, Betws-y-Coed, special attention is paid to the railways of North Wales, with dioramas showing the industry at its peak. Mangapps Railway Museum, in station buildings near Burnham-on-Crouch, houses locomotives, rolling stock and small items relating to East Anglia. The railway history of the Grampians region is portrayed in the restored Great North of Scotland Railway station at Alford, Aberdeenshire, but the development of railways on the Isle of Man is shown in the Railway Museum at Port Erin where narrow gauge, historical locomotives and carriages are included in the display. Other centres may include the work of a railway pioneer born in those parts.

Apart from those maintained by local authorities, numerous railway museums have been created by groups of enthusiasts, particularly those associated with heritage railways. Some of these are excellent in the quantity of exhibits, the high standard of restoration, and the imaginative way they are portrayed. At Shackerstone, Leicestershire on the 'Battlefield Line', one room is crammed with all kinds of memorabilia – pure nostalgia!

Before taking a closer look at a variety of named museums and centres, it is worth recalling that the LNER created the first Railway Museum in 1927 at York, to display some of the relics from the Stockton & Darlington Railway centenary celebrations of 1925. Later the range of exhibits broadened and included some locomotives from pre-Grouping companies. Those premises in Queen Street were really cramped but it was not until September 1975 that the new National Railway Museum was opened by HRH the Duke of Edinburgh.

Glasgow Transport Museum

At Kelvin Hall, Glasgow, railway exhibits are displayed alongside horse-drawn trams, traction engines, all kinds of buses, ancient cars, cycles and motorised vehicles.

The locomotives there represent a variety of styles belonging to the main Scottish railway companies, and those manufactured in Glasgow by, for example, the North British Railway Company for railways at home and overseas. Four veteran engines which were put back into good working order by BR in the late 1950s and early 1960s for the haulage of special trains were later offered for static display. These are:-

Great North of Scotland Railway 4-4-0 No. 49, built locally;

Highland Railway 4-6-0 No. 103, known as the Jones Goods, which was the first British locomotive with this wheel arrangement;

Glasgow & South Western Railway 0-6-0T No. 9, also built locally;

Caledonian Railway 4-2-2 No. 123. This 'Caledonian single' was made famous for its lively run during the Railway Races to Aberdeen in 1888. It was returned to its Caledonian blue livery prior to the Scottish Industries Fair of 1959.

The North British Railway 4-4-0 No. 256 *Glen Douglas* is on loan to the Scottish Railway Preservation Society at Bo'ness. A Caledonian 0-6-0 was loaned to the museum in 1966 but was transferred to the Strathspey Railway in 1980.

King George VI's saloon was installed in the museum in 1987 on loan from the National Railway Museum. There are of course smaller exhibits.

London Transport Museum

A similar kind of museum, depicting London Transport, is at Acton in north London. The original building in Covent Garden, which is still in use, could accommodate only a fraction of what had been saved so a reserve collection was stored at various places including Acton Underground depot. This was opened on certain days during the year until it became a museum in its own right.

The London Underground Museum at Acton has a large selection of station name boards and notices which are displayed in the gallery. (J A Wells)

The oldest exhibit is the City & South London Railway locomotive number 13, built in 1890 and used in the construction of the Underground system. There are London Transport trains showing developments over the years, most of which are in the familiar red livery though there are some interesting variations including a 1986 prototype in distinctive silver and pale green. When power to live rails was switched off during engineering work a battery locomotive was used to move the wagons: number 35 is a representative of this type. There is a large display of station names, posters, system maps, tickets and uniforms. Some 70,000 engineering drawing and numerous photographs can be consulted by arrangement. Enthusiasts who appreciate all aspects of London Transport can see a good range of buses including the open-topped General Omnibus Company vehicle of 1923 with solid tyres.

The Tanfield Railway and the Bowes Railway

The world's oldest existing railway, the Tanfield in County Durham, is a living museum, railway centre and heritage railway all in one. Along former colliery waggonways steeped in mining history, industrial tank engines from north east England trundle passengers in restored or rebuilt four-wheeled or six-wheeled carriages from the North Eastern Railway and other Victorian lines. Some of these have been used in several Catherine Cookson films for television, and represent a rare collection of vehicles over 100 years old.

Tanfield was gradually reclaimed from a derelict track bed to what is now a distance of three miles. It has a working engine shed and workshop at Marley Hill where engines, coaches and coal wagons are restored and maintained. The original colliery there, and others in the vicinity, were served by the Tanfield branch of the Brandling Junction Railway in the early 1850s. A significant part of any visit must be a ride along the line to see Causey Arch, a marvellous 102ft. single span bridge built in 1725 to carry a busy waggonway across the gorge. Today it is a pleasant, rural setting, a far cry from the once grimy, industrial scene. In addition to passenger trains visitors can see an assortment of wooden or steel coal wagons.

In its history Tanfield was in partnership with the Bowes Railway which was engineered in the 1820s by George Stephenson. In 1860 the combined line was fifteen miles long and served nine collieries. It had several cable-worked or gravity inclines and three sections worked by locomotives. Bowes ran its own passenger services from 1842, mainly for the benefit of miners.

A set of wagons begins the descent of Blackham's West incline on the preserved section of the Bowes Railway, Tyne & Wear, 2 July, 1978. (Ian S Carr)

At Springwell centre, near Gateshead, the Bowes Railway buildings are probably the most complete set of nineteenth century colliery workshops still in existence. The lengthy wagon shops, where twelve wagons could be worked on simultaneously, were originally used as a bunker to store coal awaiting transport to the quay where the loading of ships on the river Tyne depended on the state of the tide. Today they can also store locos and wagons, but an unusual, temporary conversion was as a film set depicting work in a nineteenth century match factory.

When the collieries closed most of the lines were lifted but Tyne & Wear County Council stepped in and saved a vital 1$\frac{1}{4}$ miles which included the wagon and engineering workshops, and a locomotive shed. The volunteer group has over 40 historical wagons which are used for demonstrations or left on display. Currently there are three small steam engines and four diesel shunters.

Bowes is no longer joined to the Tanfield Railway but significant are the working winding engine which hauls strings of wagons (representing loaded trucks) up the incline, and demonstrations of empty wagons in controlled descent by gravity.

The Bowes Railway is a registered Ancient Monument.

Darlington Railway Centre & Museum

Darlington Railway Museum is in the former Stockton & Darlington Railway building at North Road station. In the limited space available are the original *Locomotion* number 1 and *Derwent,* a S&DR 0-6-0 tender engine built in 1845, together with a four wheeled passenger carriage of the period. They keep company with a North Eastern Railway Fletcher 2-4-0 engine number 910, which was built at Gateshead in 1875, and number 1463, another 2-4-0, built in 1885. The latter locomotive was designed by a committee led by H Tennant, and its 7 feet 1 inch driving wheels are bigger than those of an A4 Pacific. There is also one of the sturdy 20-ton coal wagons built by the NER from 1902 and used extensively in the coal fields of the north east. The LNER continued this robust design. At the end of 1941 12,843 remained in service and seven years later 2,796 were still in regular use. Some were working in the late 50s on main lines but they could still be found in large numbers on colliery systems until the 1980s.

Ken Hoole (1916-1988) was the leading expert on the railways

A selection of builders' plates, station signs and weight restriction notices in Darlington Railway Museum. (J A Wells)

of north east England and amassed a huge collection of reference material. Following his death, this was transferred to a study centre named after him in the museum. Photographs, timetables, rule books, newspaper cuttings, maps, track diagrams, accident reports and Minutes are some of the subjects that can be consulted by prior appointment.

Inspiring as the museum and study centre are, Darlington's renowned railway fame is being resurrected a few yards away in the new Locomotive Works where an A1 Pacific is being *built from scratch,* an idea the sceptics said was impossible. The 50th locomotive of this LNER class is to be 60163 *Tornado,* named as a tribute to the RAF crews who used these fighter aircraft in the Gulf War. One nameplate carries the crest of RAF Cottesmore and the other that of the Tri-National Tornado Training Establishment based there. Both were painted by Cottesmore airmen and presented to the Trust. The Works are actually the old Stockton & Darlington Railway's Hopetown Carriage Works of 1853, another direct link with history. The A1 Locomotive Trust, with the active support of sponsors and supporters, will ensure that this project delivers a main line engine of which the country can be proud – as we are of RAF pilots! Hopefully, there are more to come from this stable.

Bressingham

The Steam Museum at Bressingham, near Diss in Norfolk is unrivalled in that not only is it privately owned but it also combines the family business of agriculture and horticulture with the owner's love of steam. Alan Bloom and his family developed Bressingham Hall gardens and surrounding land until they became the largest and most colourful of their kind in Europe. He also collected traction engines, steam rollers and lorries before turning his attention to railways – which became a major enterprise and eventually a registered charity run by a board of trustees.

At first, in 1964, a 9½-inch gauge track with a loop at each end was laid for just under half a mile. Up to twenty passengers at a time were hauled by a powerful 4-6-2 steam loco based on an LMS Princess class. The success of this miniature line encouraged the family to provide another narrow gauge run to enable visitors enjoy the pleasure of seeing expanses of colourful flowers growing further away from the Hall. The track and stock for this 2ft. wide line came from a quarry in Wales but it was in poor condition and needed a lot of attention. This Nursery Railway, as it was called, ran for half a mile past thousands of pot plants and alpines. It opened in 1966 but because of its popularity the ride is now 2½ miles long. Later the 9½-inch gauge line was replaced by an extended Garden Railway running on 10¼ gauge track, but in the meantime the Waveney Valley Railway had given visitors another choice of ride through water meadows and banks of rhododendrons. The 15-inch gauge locomotives for working this line are the German-built Pacific number 1662 *Rosenkavalier,* or 1663 *Männertreu.*

Standard gauge locomotives began to arrive at Bressingham following the construction of a large four-track engine shed in 1968. First to arrive, in deplorable condition, was the Beyer Garratt 0-4-0 0-4-0 No. 6841 *William Francis,* now the only standard gauge Garratt-type remaining in Britain. Once restored, it was a rare addition to the collection. Shortly after its arrival the former London Tilbury & Southend Railway 2-4-4T number 80 *Thundersley* was delivered, followed quickly by BR standard Britannia Pacific 70013 *Oliver Cromwell* which had taken the last steam hauled train northbound over the Settle & Carlisle a few days before. After a ¹/2 mile track had been laid the engine was used to give footplate rides. Several hundred people had enjoyed this experience before the Health & Safety inspector clamped down on the grounds of safety. 70013 was one of those from the national collection. Later, agreement was reached with Messrs Butlins to transfer from their holiday camps four locomotives they had bought from BR, which by then were showing the ravages of neglect and vandalism. Two of these were the well-known LMS 4-6-0 No. 6110 *Royal Scot* and LMS 6233 *Duchess of Sutherland.* After restoration the latter was sold to the Midland Railway Centre in 1996 and is now a certificated main line engine again.

In the museum at Bressingham, apart from the major exhibits, can be seen displays of smokebox number plates, nameplates, lamps, signalling equipment, office paperwork, full size posters, models of locomotives and general railwayana.

The work of full time staff is supplemented by volunteers who are offered a good variety of activities. The popularity of this centre can be gauged from the fact that over 95,000 visitors go there every year.

Didcot

Didcot motive power depot operated as a very busy Great Western steam shed for 121 years to 1965. It is now the home of the Great Western Society, boasting a very impressive collection of locomotives (which are housed in a four-road shed, 200 feet long), coaches, vans and wagons. To enable Didcot to replicate in part its former function, but also to broaden the experience for visitors, a purpose-built carriage shed was erected in 1977 and enlarged in 1990 to give seven tracks. In all about 40 coaches embrace suburban, main line stock and luxury saloons, some old, some replicas, and others in the process of renewal. Six of the tracks are linked to a working traverser which was originally a Midland Railway design of the 1890s used at Derby. The other line is rail connected.

Although the centre and visitor complex are open daily during the season, it is only on operating days that some of the engines are moving around the depot, using the water cranes, coaling stage and the 70ft turntable. Others are stabled around the yard. There are two short running lines. On the longer one, passenger-carrying trains shuttle back and forth for half a mile, also giving occasional demonstrations of mail exchange apparatus. To the west of the turntable is Didcot Halt with its pagoda style shelter, signal box, level crossing and nearby water tower. From there branch trains run to the north end of the site where the line ends in the transfer shed. This represents a building where goods would be exchanged between standard gauge and broad gauge stock. It is the authentic 1863 building that was moved across from Didcot goods yard. The signal box at that end is sometimes open for demonstrations of signalling.

The Society has saved a number of wagons which are being restored. These include an uncommon Royal Daylight petrol tanker, a fish van (code named Bloater), vans for flour, a tar wagon, pairs of six-wheeled bogies for carrying long girders, and a six-wheeled van for prize cattle. In the museum area the display of railwayana is as excellent as it is diverse. The whole place just oozes Great Western!

The return from Australia of 4079 *Pendennis Castle* in July 2000 (to where it had been taken by a mining company 23 years before) and its donation to the GW Society was a great boost. Members and friends, with help from the National Lottery, raised the cash to pay for its passage from exile. 4079 is now under restoration for main line running, probably by 2004.

A replica of a Firefly class broad gauge engine is currently being built at Didcot and it is hoped to rebuild *Maindy Hall* as *Lady of Legend*, number 999, to fill a gap in the locomotive fleet – a Saint class. For the millennium celebrations the Society displayed 2,000 locomotives including many models in different scales. The real *Flying Scotsman* and *Blue Peter* were there representing the LNER.

Barrow Hill

Barrow Hill at Staveley, Chesterfield, was a red brick Midland Railway engine shed where 24 'roads' radiated from a central turntable. It became a diesel depot in 1965 but following its closure by BR in 1991 the fabric of the building quickly deteriorated and there was a real chance that it would be demolished. The whole vandalised site was bought by Chesterfield Council six years later who, with the enthusiastic co-operation of Barrow Hill Engine Shed Society and some financial help from grants, achieved a high quality restoration of the 1870 depot. It is now a working roundhouse, the only one in the country, and a Grade Two listed building.

It was ten years before restoration was complete but the official opening in July 1998 made all the work worthwhile. Four locomotives with Midland Railway connections were transported in for the occasion but the one taking the leading role and returning to its home shed was the Johnson 1F 'half-cab' number 41708 0-6-0T. A 96-year-old driver who had worked at the shed for 45 years before he retired in 1963 was thrilled to be invited.

At an open day the following year, Stanier Jubilee class No. 45593 *Kolhapur* and Stanier 8F No. 48305 were included in the visiting engines; then in the year 2000, the shed's 130th anniversary, ten steam engines were taken in from various centres after resident diesels had been moved out of the shed for the occasion. At the end of the day eight engines coupled together, seven of them in steam, were run slowly into the shed from the yard outside, turned one at a time on the turntable and parked up. Owners of heritage steam, diesel or electric traction have used the centre to restore their acquisitions. The first main line diesels to make Barrow Hill their permanent home were 45060 and 37111. There are plans to extend the length of run outside the roundhouse and to build a conventional shed. At present the steam gala is an annual event.

National Railway Museum, York

We come now to the ultimate railway museum, a visit to which is essential for anyone interested in railways.

Although strong objections were made in some quarters when it was proposed to move the Railway Museum from London to the former York North motive power depot, there can be no doubt that the new museum very quickly established itself as a centre of excellence, a foundation on which it has continued to build. British Rail re-constructed the basic edifice, moved in the

*A short section of broad gauge track at the National Railway Museum allows 4-2-2 **Iron Duke** to be run on certain days. 50003, alongside, carries the large double-arrow symbol. (K Morton)*

larger exhibits, then passed it over to the Science Museum, London, for day-to-day administration. The first exhibits to be relocated were the locomotive *Argenoria* (1829) and a Stockton & Darlington Railway coach, which were transported from the original building in York.

Having the legal power to claim any object no longer of use to the nationalised railway, it is inevitable that the National Railway Museum has constantly expanded over the last 25 years. With more than 100 locomotives, 167 coaches and wagons from the earliest days, twelve Royal Train vehicles, a fabulous collection of nameplates, trackwork, signals, horse-drawn vehicles – and demonstrating by the use of modern technology how things used to be done – there is little wonder this museum is known for having the finest collections in any country. The steam locomotives include such famous names as *Rocket, Hardwicke, City of Truro, Gladstone, Green Arrow* and *Mallard.* In 1988 *Mallard* was prepared for a short season of main line running to commemorate the 50th anniversary of her speed record. The 0-4-2 locomotive *Gladstone,* originally owned by the London Brighton & South Coast Railway, was bought from the Southern Railway in 1927 by the Stephenson Locomotive Society. Those on display are in pristine condition externally. For the first fifteen years the museum maintained a number of engines to provide power for steam specials but this was curtailed in favour of presenting the story of railways to a more general public.

In 1990, when the main building had to be closed for reroofing, a decision was taken to remove one of the two remaining turntables (howls of protest – there used to be four!) Some of the main exhibits were transferred to the former York Central Goods Depot on the other side of the road; the rest were put on temporary display at Swindon or dispersed on loan to bona fide groups. On completion of the work both sections of the museum were joined by a subway.

After four years of planning and construction, things changed again in 1999 with the opening of what has been termed The Works. What used to be the diesel depot, alongside the steam shed, had been used for overhauling and restoring locomotives away from the gaze of visitors to the museum. Now, after alterations, a new gallery enables the public to see what is going on in the workshop below which there are three tracks. Coaches, cranes and a heavy snowplough are among the items rebuilt so far. Still upstairs and overlooking the east coast main line, five display screens with track diagrams duplicate the whole area controlled from the York signalling centre. It is possible to watch on the screens the progress of every train on the main line and on routes to Leeds, Scarborough and Harrogate. By contrast, the block system of controlling the movement of trains can also be demonstrated. Just outside is a balcony giving an unrestricted view of the north end of the station, a very popular innovation of the extended museum.

The warehouse section, which has enabled another 5,000 exhibits to be made available, is more spartan than the main display areas. Facing visitors as they make their way along this section is the large sculpture of Britannia which once graced Euston. There are over 100 small crates that contain a huge assortment of labelled exhibits; elsewhere around the floor are numerous railway 'bits and pieces' (all fascinating) together with more locomotives and stock, some of which may one day be given cosmetic restoration. One craftsman model maker bequeathed 600 London & North Western Railway vehicles he had made over the years, a historical display in themselves. The foregoing is a mere hint of some of the NRM's treasures which are said to number 3/4 million.

The library at the National Railway Museum has some 15,000 volumes, 600 different journal titles, many thousands of photographs, engineering drawings, diagrams, posters, leaflets, an enormous number of timetables . . . the list could go on! As space in the reading room is limited, people who wish to carry out research (or even just browse around the magazines, photofiles or reference books on display) need to telephone for an appointment to book a space for a day or half a day. The writer has always found the staff to be very helpful and as far as possible they have the material you wish to consult to hand for when you arrive. Unfortunately some people expect the staff to do all their research for them, which is just not possible.

The National Archive of Railway Oral History has been established at York with a view to recording for posterity interviews with former employees in many areas of the industry. A joint initiative between the NRM and the University of York in 1995 established the Institute of Railway Studies, leading to a degree.

In the year 2000 plans were announced for a massive expansion at York on recently acquired land. Furthermore it is hoped to develop a 60,000 sq.ft. annexe on part of the former marshalling yard at Shildon, County Durham, not far from the Timothy Hackworth Museum.

It is worth noting that at least one open weekend a year is staged at one of the major rail depots or works in which modern locomotives, multiple units and visiting steam engines are on display, supplemented by exhibitions (e.g. nameplates) and trade stands. Thousands of enthusiastic people attend each event and the money raised is donated to charity. Details are advertised in railway magazines.

This chapter is just a glimpse at the alluring world of railway museums which offer such a wide variety of approach to railway studies.

WYLAM   WHERE RAILWAYS WERE BORN

BICENTENARY OF 1781–1981 GEORGE STEPHENSON

Part of the commemorative envelope. Note the caption on the seal – "Never Give Up". (See opposite page).

GEORGE STEPHENSON BICENTENARY 1781-1981

Wylam Celebrations Tuesday 9th June 1981

OFFICIAL PROGRAMME
for the opening of the
Wylam Railway Museum
and treeplanting ceremony
at Stephenson's Cottage
to commemorate the
200th anniversary of
George Stephenson's
birth.

At the celebrations to mark the bicentenary of George Stephenson's birth, guests were invited to the Official Opening of Wylam Railway Museum and to attend a tree planting ceremony at the cottage where he lived.

TRAFFIC FIGURES FOR TOTNES, PLYMOUTH DIVISION

	1903	1913	1923	1933
PASSENGER TRAIN TRAFFIC				
Tickets Issued	64,761	64,019	58,808	39,026
Season Tickets	n.a.	n.a.	358	217
Parcels & Miscellaneous (number)	36,612	38,121	41,131	48,481
**GOODS TRAFFIC FORWARDED **				
Coal & Coke Charged (tons)	16	--	--	18
Other Minerals (tons)	64	35	128	162
General Merchandise (tons)	3,586	3,856	3,245	3,126
**GOODS TRAFFIC RECEIVED **				
Coal & Coke Charged (tons)	1,260	622	400	2,710
Other minerals (tons)	509	2,413	444	1,455
General Merchandise (tons)	7,247	7,958	6,414	6,041
COAL & COKE NOT CHARGED (tons) *Forwarded and Received*	528	1,728	3,157	3,370
LIVESTOCK *Forwarded and Received* (wagons)	514	990	853	128
TOTAL CARTAGE TONNAGE	4,817	5,202	5,242	5,412

** Includes Totnes Quay and Rattery.

(Extracted from 'Traffic Dealt with at Stations and Goods Depots, G.W.R.' National Railway Museum)

Chapter Eleven
HERITAGE RAILWAYS
(Originally known as Preserved Railways)

You may have been to a local tourist office, a hotel or guest house and seen leaflets or posters advertising a steam railway within easy travelling distance or perhaps further afield, and you decide to make a visit. Your first impression will probably be of a well run organisation, with helpful staff and a real sense of purpose. In the year of the millennium there were more than 150 heritage railways, varying greatly in size, length of run and in what was offered. Each one is different in character, location and complexity, yet collectively they reflect the complex operating and safety standards used by railway companies for many decades.

Former colliery engines, at Goathland on the North Yorkshire Moors Railway in 1970. 0-6-2T number 5 is still working hard up the gradient as it pulls into the station; but 29 is undergoing restoration. (Ian S. Carr)

Typical standard gauge lines have one or more platforms – some connected by a footbridge – with station buildings which include the booking office. There are authentic notices, enamel signs advertising Oxo, Zebo grate polish, and chocolate (among others), barrows with luggage or milk churns, genuine lamps, and flower beds. There are locomotives and coaches, parcel vans and wagons. Engines will have an appropriate livery with correct markings and using headlamp codes according to the class of train. An express passenger, for example, has a lamp above each of the leading buffers, a stopping passenger train has a single lamp below the chimney (or equivalent position on the tender or coal bunker); an engine running 'light' (on its own or with just a brake van) has one lamp in the centre of the buffer beam. If the station is a terminus the process of uncoupling, running round the train and recoupling can be watched. Each train must carry a tail lamp on the last vehicle to show signalmen the train is complete. There are of course the usual signals which are interlocked in the signal box to prevent conflicting movements.

Such an ordered routine belies at least ten years of struggle and a constant battle to get the system up and running – so how did it start?

In the late 1940s and throughout the 1950s and 60s train spotting was a popular hobby, with enthusiastic groups on platforms at every main line station. They were surrounded by railway sights and sounds – the hiss of steam and the characteristic exhaust of different classes of locomotive, the slamming of carriage doors, engine whistles, the odd wheel-slip, the clickety-click of wheels over rail joints and their complaining screech on tight curves, and strings of barrows loaded with parcels. Above all there was the thrill of 'copping a namer'. Following the Beeching axe and the forthcoming end of steam, alarm bells began to ring among enthusiasts. For the country that had introduced railways to the world, trains as we had known them could not be allowed to disappear! Numerous meetings were held in homes, pubs and church halls; there were embryonic discussions on golf courses and elsewhere but the message was clear – WE MUST SAVE OUR RAILWAYS.

Requests were made to rent or buy redundant lines from British Rail. If sufficient deposits could be raised in time the rails were left intact, otherwise the demolition gangs moved in. In the early days industrial locomotives gave brake van rides along a few hundred yards of track before surplus coaches became available. These enabled the aim of running trains in an authentic manner with steam or diesel locomotives to be fulfilled. Hundreds of steam engines were cut up but those bought for scrap by Dai Woodham at Barry in south Wales were left untouched for some years. These rusting, cannibalised wrecks were eventually rescued and many were rebuilt! Some lines bought locomotives from overseas.

Where did the money come from for these prodigious schemes? Local councils often gave valuable support, but share schemes, donations, legacies, membership fees, and numerous fund-raising events, together with help from the National Lottery and other sources, have all played their part. Major lines offer engine driving courses, and galas featuring steam or diesel traction, or both – even 'wartime weekends' – are held regularly. Dining trains, sometimes composed of Pullman stock, are very popular. What could be better than an unhurried trip along the line and a leisurely meal with the train at rest out in the beautiful countryside? Mention must also be made of the excellent and informative in-house magazines produced by many groups. Although it is an anathema to many people, Thomas the Tank Engine weekends certainly bring in much needed cash. These engines with faces are based on the characters in the favourite children's books originally written by the Rev Awdrey and which became an acclaimed television series.

Apart from drivers, firemen, guards and booking clerks, staff are needed in the refreshment rooms, the shop, for cleaning coaches, repairing and renovating stock, maintaining track and signals, and general day to day organisation. There are some paid officials but a tremendous amount of work is done by volunteers, often in far from favourable conditions. They come from all sections of the community. An ideal way to extend ones knowledge of railways is to become involved. Helpers are always needed and training is given. It is not all plain sailing however, as various projects have had to cope with floods, landslips, vandalism, thieving, even arson. Imagine the feeling of frustration and anger on seeing months or even years of patient restoration of a vehicle reduced to ashes.

Some railways which have a proven track record have been entrusted with locomotives from the national collection where in return for a complete restoration to the highest standards, the line is allowed to run the engine for a given period up to ten years. The Great Central Railway has completed the reconstruction of the former O4 class 2-8-0, number 63601, built in 1911 and withdrawn in 1964. The engineer in charge of this exciting project was only 25 years of age at the time. Privately owned locomotives to be used on the national network have to be fitted with spark arresters and are subject to very stringent and costly inspections.

Some schemes slid into oblivion but others have gone from strength to strength, extending their range. More projects are in hand to join what is now a multi-million pound industry.

To conclude this brief review of heritage railways let us look at the variety available by using five as examples.

The Bo'ness & Kinneil Railway

It is quite common for people to collect model railway locomotives and rolling stock but have no layout on which to run them. Translate this into actual railways where individuals or groups own real engines, coaches and wagons which they carefully restore – then have to be content with them as static exhibits. This was the dilemma of the Scottish Railway Preservation Society, which was formed in 1961 with the aim of acquiring and displaying relics of the Scottish railways, then, hopefully running some of them.

In the early days its members were allowed by British Rail to rent the former tranship shed at Springfield goods yard in Falkirk, where exhibits were put on show. As the Society obtained locomotives, rolling stock and artefacts, and its good name became known, many more items were loaned or donated from various sources. This base was closed in 1987 as the location was to be part of a development programme. Meanwhile there had been a glimmer of hope. In the 1950s there was a junction at Manuel on the Edinburgh to Glasgow main line which led to Bo'ness harbour. This had been a very busy port on the Firth of Forth handling mainly coal, timber and iron ore but with numerous sidings providing secondary traffic from factories and works. When the area became redundant it left a large expanse of derelict land that was unsuitable for redevelopment, so that when a plan for a major tourist attraction based on a new railway system at Bo'ness was put forward it received eager support from Falkirk Council.

In 1979 the SRPS began to create a heritage railway from virtually nothing, as much of the track and infrastructure of the former branch had been removed, but within two years the empty site alongside the dock basin had been transformed and a working steam railway established. The Bo'ness & Kinneil Railway, 3 1/2 miles in length, was opened in style in 1981. The new station building at Bo'ness was constructed to represent a typical North British style. The smaller 1887 station building from Wormit, at the southern end of the Tay bridge where a train plunged into the water during a severe storm in 1879, was renovated and erected nearby to give larger premises. The footbridge was brought from the Highland Railway main line to Inverness, whereas the signal box originated on the Caledonian Railway near Coatbridge. Another notable exhibit erected at Bo'ness was the 1842 trainshed roof and supporting columns which came from Edinburgh's Haymarket station, at one time the terminus of the Edinburgh & Glasgow Railway. There are also working gas lamps. The Scottish Railway Exhibition on the site shows how the railways carried their traffic – but things are moving forward and there are ambitious plans to extend the whole area to become eventually the largest railway preservation centre in the UK.

Among the locomotives is the restored Caledonian Railway 0-4-4T number 419, a sturdy favourite once used on suburban routes and branch lines. A Holmes J36 0-6-0 number 65243 *Maude* (originally North British No. 673) was one of 50 engines of this class to see service in France during World War I. They were named after military leaders, or places associated with the war zone. The motive power stock is enhanced by a BR standard class 4 2-6-4T number 80105, once a virtual wreck. Visiting engines have included J72 69023 and K1 2-6-0 number 2005 owned by the North Eastern Locomotive Preservation Group, NELPG for short.

*Restored to its original condition on the Bo'ness & Kinneil Railway, North British 0-6-0 **Maude**, number 673, worked in France in World War I. (K Morton)*

The SRPS owns a fine rake of maroon coaches which are used for charter work on the national network.

Between 1986 and 1988 the south end of the line was at Kinneil Halt, then an extension was opened to Birkhill. Although it is not in regular use, the track does continue for about a mile to Manuel where it joins the main line. It is planned to build a terminus there in due course. The Society's collection has over twenty steam locomotives and as many diesels, over 50 coaches and 200+ wagons or works vehicles, which will keep the restoration groups very busy for years to come.

The Keighley & Worth Valley Railway

This Midland Railway branch line was opened in 1867 between Oxenhope and Keighley, where it joined the Leeds to Settle and Carlisle main line. Five miles in length and in rugged moorland, it served the numerous textile mills and factories of the Worth Valley. It passed through the village of Haworth, famed as the home of the Brontë family. The last passenger train ran at the end of 1961 and BR closed the branch shortly afterwards. Local residents met within weeks and the Keighley & Worth Valley Preservation Society was established. It has the distinction of running steam trains every weekend since passenger services were restored on the private railway in June 1968, following certification by the Railway Inspectorate.

Keighley station, with its long, glazed canopy and numerous hanging baskets in summer, has an air of importance. Worth Valley trains use one of the platforms and have run-round facilities. At the south end of the station is a turntable that originally came from Garsdale, the one which is known for rotating in a gale with an engine on board and could not be stopped until the wind abated! After that a stockade was built to give some protection.

At Ingrow (West) the once derelict station has been completely rebuilt. It is the home base of the Bahamas Locomotive Society; also of the Vintage Carriages Trust whose outstanding restorations have won many accolades and awards. Two of these are a four-wheeled composite coach of the Great Central Railway dating from 1876 and a Great Northern six-wheeler built in 1888.

Damems is thought to be the smallest standard gauge station in the country. Oakworth, another meticulously renovated station, was used as the filming location for the original version of

'The Railway Children' which generated enormous publicity and thousands of visitors – not forgetting a useful cheque from the film company. Several other preserved lines have been used in this way, notably the North Yorkshire Moors Railway where railway scenes for the popular 'Heartbeat' series on television were enacted.

At Haworth the former goods shed is now used as the engine shed and workshop area. Other locomotives awaiting attention are stored at Oxenhope, the terminus.

The K&WVR brought together an enviable collection of locomotives and rolling stock in all sorts of conditions. Even those that appeared to be lost causes were painstakingly restored to working order as funds allowed. A wonderful variety of steam engines has been seen on the branch, including those on loan from other sources and some which have stayed a few days between main line duties. The oldest resident is an 0-6-0 well tank – the water tanks are between the frames – but this is only one of several distinctive industrial locomotives. The K&WVR does participate in exchange schemes which are to mutual benefit. There is a good selection of coaches and a variety of goods wagons, some of which are used on demonstration freights or for groups of photographers. Parcel vans, or similar, include a Gresley full brake, four-wheeled Southern covered carriage trucks with opening end doors, and general utility vans used originally for mail, parcels and luggage. The wagons are types such as blue-spot fish vans, tankers, a 'Lowmac', flat wagons, covered vans including one for carrying bananas, and brake vans. There is a 'Walrus' for carrying ballast, a 'Shark' ballast plough, and cranes. One of the latter is a 50-ton breakdown crane that had been used in the clearance of several major derailments during its service.

The railway not only provides a fascinating location for enthusiasts, it is also used frequently by local people.

The Railway Preservation Society of Ireland

This Railway Preservation Society, formed in 1964, embraces both Northern Ireland and the Irish Republic. Its aim was to preserve in working order some locomotives and coaches before they all disappeared from the railway scene and were lost for ever. The Society moved into its headquarters at Whitehead, on the coast to the north east of Belfast, in 1966 and opened a depot at Mullingar, to the north west of Dublin, eight years later.

The RPSI has preserved eight locomotives to date of which half would normally be available for duty. There are two former Great Southern & Western Railway 0-6-0s, class 101 (later J15) built in 1879 and 1880. Two 4-4-0s are used on passenger trains; both worked on the Great Northern Railway (Ireland). Number 171 *Slieve Gullion* (1913) is a popular performer but number 85 *Merlin*, on loan from the Ulster Folk & Transport Museum, has only recently been returned to traffic after a major overhaul. The Dublin & South Eastern Railway's 2-6-0 number 461 was out of use for 30 years before its return to traffic. It is worth mentioning that their LMS 2-6-4T was bought for £1,275.

In the Society's collection of coaches, a twelve-wheeled gas-lit brake composite built in 1906 for the Rosslare Boat Express rubs buffers with examples of good designs from the 1920s through to the 1950s. In all there are 33 carriages with twenty or so passed for use on the main line. Some of the others need a lot of attention because of their poor condition.

About a dozen main line trips are organised each year. The 'Portrush Flyer' runs from Belfast to Portrush; the 'Atlantic Coast Express' goes to Londonderry, and in summer the 'Sea Breeze' runs between Dublin and Rosslare Harbour. There are other one-day excursions from Dublin, and of course Santa Specials, all advertised in railway magazines and elsewhere. For these outings the Society uses an eight-coach train of restored vintage stock and enjoys a high level of co-operation from Northern Ireland Railways and Iarnrod Eireann.

Twenty-two wagons and vans of different kinds have been acquired but the state of most of them is only poor-to-fair. Six 'rail wagons', converted from former passenger coaches, are in traffic.

The Railway Preservation Society of Ireland has won several awards over the years for its activities in railway preservation and the development of tourism. Without the efforts of these people the only reminders of steam locomotives would have been in museums.

The Welshpool & Llanfair Light Railway

Apart from a primitive, horse-worked line built in 1817 to transport stone from a quarry to a canal a short distance away, it was the Oswestry & Newtown Railway that first brought a railway to the ancient market town of Welshpool though the operating side was provided by Cambrian Railways. When a proposal to build a line from Llanfair Caereinion to Welshpool was agreed it was decided that a gauge of two feet six inches would be used, an unusual and uncommon choice. Construction started in 1901, with the route twisting, climbing and dipping for a distance of nine scenic miles. Goods traffic commenced in 1904, followed by passenger trains in 1905.

As with many schemes, capital in the early days was in very short supply. The company purchased three coaches but could not afford a fourth; even the first timber trucks were bought on hire purchase. Cambrian Railways continued to run the line until Grouping when it became part of the Great Western Railway. The new owner introduced a bus service between Llanfair and Welshpool so inevitably passenger trains were withdrawn, early in 1931, leaving the transportation of coal, agricultural produce, building material, cattle, sheep and timber as the main traffic. By the time of Nationalisation in 1948 all this had been significantly reduced. Closure, it seemed, was inevitable.

Before the fateful day – in November 1956 – enthusiasts and well wishers had joined forces and approached British Rail with a request that they should be allowed to rent the railway, the first time such an idea had been considered. There followed a period of inactivity during which the condition of the infrastructure and stock deteriorated. Nevertheless, following agreement with BR, there was a steely determination to rebuild and run the railway, initially from Llanfair to Castle Caereinion. After 32 years the first passenger train squirmed over the line using coaches obtained from the Admiralty following the closure of its Lodge Hill & Upnor Railway, but as these vehicles were not fitted with vacuum brakes they were subsequently disposed of. The horizon of a full reopening was a little nearer!

Restoration and progress continued as funds permitted until eventually in 1981 the rest of the neglected track had been relaid to reach a new station at Welshpool. This section included the formidable Golpha incline, nearly a mile of 1 in 29. 6,500 hardwood sleepers imported from Australia were laid together with huge amounts of new ballast. So what might a visitor see today now that this line is owned by the Welshpool & Llanfair Light Railway?

Without doubt, a big attraction is the heterogeneous collection of locomotives which are larger than normal for narrow gauge because of the severe gradients. Some of these have been brought in from Austria, Antigua, Sierra Leone and Finland. All those in traffic are well turned out. Again, because of the gauge, coaches were obtained from overseas: five four-wheeled vehicles with end balconies were donated by the Zillertalbahn in Austria. Three other bogie coaches which had been built at Gloucester were returned from Sierra Leone. They had originally been supplied as a gift to mark the country's independence in 1961.

Goods wagons from various sources are closed vans, open wagons, a bogie well wagon built in the company's workshops, and brake vans. Stations have been rebuilt, adapted, or brought in from elsewhere and look very smart. A locomotive shed, machine shops, gift shops, tearoom and car parks complete the scene, justifying the dreams of the people who refused to let this railway die. It is also a tribute to the manufacturer, Beyer Peacock, that two of the original engines from 1902 – *The Earl* and *Countess* – are still able to work with the other five steam and three diesel locomotives.

The West Somerset Railway

To conclude this snapshot of heritage railways let us pay a visit to a thoroughbred Great Western line which meanders and climbs through the fields and woodlands between Minehead on the coast of the Bristol Channel and Bishops Lydeard near Taunton. It is the West Somerset Railway. It is the longest heritage line, stretching for twenty miles, but there is an additional three miles to give a direct link with what is now the western main line. In all there are ten stations, some of which provide passing places on the single track line. This is the home of Manor class engines, of panniers and prairies, lower quadrants signals and chocolate and cream paintwork – a typical west country branch!

Before final closure of the line to Minehead by British Rail in 1971 there had been moves to purchase the whole branch and run it as a private company to provide commuter services and steam trains aimed at attracting visitors to the area. Picking out the bare bones from hours of discussion, planning and aspirations, a volunteer support group was formed and a Light Railway Order was granted in 1974. Facing months of hard work, volunteers embarked on restoring stations, relaying track, reinstating signals, removing weeds and in general preparing to be operational. The first trains ran over part of the line in July 1975, then in March of the following year the first section from Minehead through Dunster to Blue Anchor was officially opened by Lord Montagu of Beaulieu. Within five months the half-way point had been reached with the extension of the line to Williton. The remainder, including the three-mile section to Norton Fitzwarren, was ready for use in June 1979. The slogan used by the company, 'Better by Miles', is very apt.

The original station at Minehead was opened in 1874 but was altered and enlarged several times as traffic changed. The main platform can accommodate a thirteen-coach train. There is a two-road engine shed and in 1992 a purpose built carriage shed was erected. The former goods shed is now part of the locomotive engineering workshops.

At Williton the platforms are noticeably further apart, giving a reminder that this branch was laid to broad gauge standards. The Diesel & Electric Preservation Group is based there so it is appropriate that most of the diesel fleet, including the Western Region diesel hydraulics, is stored at this station. Steam engines are overhauled or restored in a separate building.

Washford has several sidings to stable coaches and wagons. Most of the coaches in regular use are former BR mark 1s dating from the 1950s. Goods wagons are used mainly on open days and for charter freight trains. The small museum features artefacts from the former Somerset & Dorset Railway, one of the companies that became part of the GWR in 1923. The main museum however is at Blue Anchor which is crammed with Great Western and west country railwayana. In the signal box there the level crossing gates are still turned by the traditional large gate wheel. Nearby are three GWR coaches from 1917, now used as accommodation for volunteers working on the railway.

Over the years a wide variety of locomotives has operated on the WSR, predominantly Great Western, British Railways standard types or BR Western region. Up to a dozen ex-BR engines are based on this line but, as with other heritage railways, not all are in service at any one time, indeed some have to be stored for a considerable period awaiting attention. Visitors to the branch have included *Evening Star, City of Truro, Duke of Gloucester, Clun Castle, Swanage* and *Taw Valley.*

The company regularly runs the popular dining train known as the 'Quantock Belle'; Santa specials and 'Thomas weekends' are also regular features. Charter trains, including high speed 125s run occasionally through to Minehead. By contrast, EWS diesel locomotives have conveyed train loads of very large pieces of rock quarried in the Mendip Hills for use in the construction of new defences against the sea at Minehead. The ambience of this line with its award winning stations and beautiful countryside makes it another ideal location for film makers. Altogether this is a purposeful, working railway providing wide-ranging interests for its visitors and satisfaction (but ongoing challenges) for its supporters. It is recorded that in the year 2000 season, 33,600 tea bags and 2^{1}/$_{4}$ hundredweight of coffee were used representing 66,000 cups in total – which shows they make a good, hot 'cuppa' too!

Chapter Twelve
ADDITIONAL SOURCES OF INFORMATION
(I)
ACCIDENT REPORTS TO MAGAZINES
ACCIDENT REPORTS

As far back as 1840 suitably qualified army officers holding the rank of captain or above were engaged to thoroughly investigate railway accidents where death or injuries had occurred. Their reports pinpointed the causes and made recommendations to improve safety. These were not always accepted favourably by railway company chairmen, some of whom were openly hostile. It was only when Parliament stipulated what had to be done and enforced it by law that the changes were introduced. After the Newark brake trials in 1875, for example, continuous brakes were quickly fitted to most British passenger stock. The Act of 1889, which made such brakes compulsory, was passed to ensure obstinate companies conformed.

These elite army officers, who were well respected for their knowledge of railway operation, also inspected new lines before passenger trains were allowed to run, making return visits where necessary.

The causes of railway accidents over the years have been many and varied. In the early days trains were permitted to follow one another at intervals of five to ten minutes as a general rule. This time interval system worked satisfactorily provided a train did not break down, hit an obstruction on the track, or stall on a gradient – otherwise it could be run into by a following train. This was known as a rear end collision. Coming across a disabled train just round a bend, hidden by trees, would not give a driver time to stop. Apart from that there were no compulsory eyesight tests in those days!

Two specific accidents will serve as illustrations of errors by signalmen and a driver. Imagine for a moment the scene at Quintinshill, on the Caledonian Railway, ten miles north of Carlisle shortly after 6 a.m. on the morning of 22nd May 1915. The two main lines with crossover points between them each had a loop running alongside. A local passenger train heading north had to make way for the Scotch express which consisted of thirteen bogie coaches including West Coast Joint Stock sleeping cars. It had left Carlisle just over thirty minutes late. As the Down loop (northbound) was already occupied by a goods train of 45 loaded wagons, the local was backed through the crossover onto the Up main – an accepted practice – and stood less than 60 yards from the signal box, in full view. Very soon afterwards a train of empty coal wagons returning to Wales was run into the Up loop because there was no room for it at Kingmoor. Being 'put inside' would also clear the way for a southbound troop train which should have passed once the local passenger train had resumed its journey and left the Up main line clear. Three trains were then standing there leaving only the Down main clear, and on which the express would pass. Forgetting about the local train, one of the signalmen (they were changing shifts at the time) accepted the troop special and pulled off his signals to indicate the line was clear. Approaching at a high speed on a falling gradient, it smashed into the local train scattering debris in all directions. Although some attempts were made to stop it, minutes later the northbound express hauled by two engines ploughed into the wreckage, running into and killing soldiers who were escaping from the first collision. The carnage was compounded by wooden coaches lit by gas, which was ignited by burning coals from the engines. The fire spread rapidly. 227 people lost their lives though there may have been more as lists of service personnel on the trains were destroyed.

The very comprehensive report by Lt. Col. Druitt shows the actions carried out in the emergency by drivers, firemen, brakesmen and others were in accordance with regulations. It gave full details of how rescue work was organised, including the help given by the survivors of the troop train under the guidance of their officers, and similarly by the navy people from the express. The blame for this terrible tragedy was laid firmly on the shoulders of both signalmen for developing a lack of discipline and working in a lax manner by neglecting to follow the various rules which had been framed to prevent such horrors. If track circuits, which show when a section of track is occupied, had been installed at Quintinshill it would not have been possible to clear the signals, though these were not usually put in where the signalman had a good view. More simply, a lever collar would have reminded the signalmen of a standing train, but they did not bother to use one.

An accident at the beginning of World War II, in the blackout, happened on a wet, windy and very dark night at Norton Fitzwarren in November 1940 when a sleeping car express from Paddington to Penzance was derailed. Having called at Taunton, the express would normally have continued its journey on the main line but on this occasion, because it was running late and had lost its allocated 'path', it was routed along the adjacent relief line so that a lightly loaded newspaper train could dash through the station on the main.

The driver of the express mistook the green signal as being for his train and continued to accelerate, at the same time passing two signals at danger. At the end of the relief line the two tracks converged – but there were run-off points (also called catch points, or 'jacks') which would derail a train unless the points were set to join the main line. The two trains ran side by side until the newspaper train pulled ahead. Realising his mistake when he saw a train on his right side, the driver of the express braked sharply just as the safety points did the job for which they were designed, with ruthless efficiency. As the engine plunged into the earth and fell on its side, the first six coaches scattered across the four tracks with terrible consequences. 26 people died and many more were injured. Had the newspaper train been just a few seconds later it would have crashed into the wreckage. In recent years safety points have been removed from many locations, probably on the assumption that the few times they would prevent an accident was not worth the expense of maintaining them.

Reports such as these are a very useful source of information in that they provide an insight into railway operation apart from giving facts about specific mishaps. They contain information about the site, supplemented by detailed diagrams where these can illustrate the track layout, location of buildings, distances, signal posts, and the position of vehicles. The condition of the track, gradients, damage sustained, and indentations or twisting caused by wheels were all carefully noted. The make up of each train was recorded, its length, weight, brakes, and often the damage to each vehicle. The inspector would want to know that all checks had been made before the train left its depot. In addition the visibility of signals from the moving footplate had to be taken into consideration. Did bridges, buildings or trees obscure the view, particularly on curves?

The causes of the accident were declared and comments made about the weather conditions and light. Interviews with staff were included, particular attention being given when it was felt that there was a plot to 'cover up' for colleagues. Copies of accident reports can be consulted at relevant main libraries and record offices but centres like the PRO at Kew and the National Railway Museum have copies of most of them, or they can be obtained from HM Stationery Office.

When people are killed in rail accidents the safety of trains is called into question by the media, sometimes to the point of hysteria. Whilst there is total sympathy for the victims and their families it is necessary to look at the overall picture to view the statistics in perspective. Between 1976 and 1998 there were *nine years in which no passenger was killed in a railway accident.* In the period from 1990 to 1998 there were fifteen passenger deaths, but in that time the *railways carried about seven billion passengers* ('Steel Wheels'). By contrast, in *1999 alone 3,564 people were killed on the roads of the United Kingdom, 143 more than the previous year.* That increase alone is higher than any continuous ten year period for rail passengers. ('Railway Magazine': P Semmens).

The duties of the Railway Inspectorate changed little until the early 1990s when it was taken over by the Health & Safety Executive. Following vocal calls for an independent Railway Accident Investigation Unit, the report of Lord Cullen into the Ladbroke Grove crash of October 1999 has endorsed this recommendation.

ACTS OF PARLIAMENT

All proposals to build, extend or amalgamate railways had to be agreed by Parliament – but a great deal of preparatory work was needed before events reached that stage.

Land owners, industrialists, farmers, fishermen and business men are some of the people who could benefit from having a railway near at hand. Initial ideas would be discussed in homes or local hostelries and the general reaction would be tested before an official meeting was called. If the consensus was to go forward a committee would be formed and a chairman elected.

It was always a great advantage to have the support of a leading personality, someone with 'position' or authority and with influential friends. The next step would be a detailed survey of the proposed route and the preparation of a prospectus that would give details of the scheme and emphasise its importance to the community. Promises of financial support would be sought by indicating the potential returns from investing in the railway. Many people would be speculators seeking to 'make a quick buck'.

The prospectus would be presented to Parliament as a Bill and be considered by a select committee. Over days or weeks its members would question the presenters in detail, seeking clarification, confirmation or sometimes confrontation. Frequently landowners, other railway companies, and individuals or groups would oppose such a Bill. Both sides would have their arguments presented by a barrister and expert witnesses would be called. The decision could go either way. If the project was rejected the supporters could try again at a later date. If agreed, various stipulations were laid down relating to such things as capital, borrowing, charges for traffic, the number of directors, general organisation and the target date for completion. These details were spelt out in the Act. The powers given were formidable and permitted the compulsory purchase of land and buildings, the acquisition of rights of way, and diverting roads, canals, tramways, sewers and drains. The company could cross on the level, or go over or under any road or railway along its proposed route.

Copies of Acts of Parliament can be consulted at appropriate libraries or record offices, or obtained from the House of Commons library.

CHARTER TRAINS

Back in Pre-Grouping days a day out was often a trip to the seaside. Railway companies advertised excursions by posters, handbills, or in the press, and these were very popular. One arranged by the Blyth & Tyne Railway in 1861 for a distance of less than fifteen miles carried 1,408 passengers. The railways were happy to provide trains for organisations like schools, and when companies took their employees and their families away for their annual 'trip'. Other 'specials' were arranged for theatre visits, football matches, horse racing, exhibitions and selected events. This pattern has been continued up to present times, modified as necessary, so it is worth while looking at charter operations today.

Specialist travel firms arrange out and back tours to popular destinations like York, Stratford-upon-Avon, and Edinburgh, giving people several hours in the place they are visiting. Passengers may sometimes be given a choice of two or three destinations fairly close together to cater for different interests. Some may want to visit a cathedral city, others prefer shopping, or visiting a preserved railway or museum a few miles away. Alternatively, the tour may be one where most of the time is spent travelling rather than visiting. Special tours are arranged for railway enthusiasts which may involve the use of different diesel locomotives working singly or in pairs and covering routes not normally visited by charter trains. Nevertheless, the days of very early starts, complex itineraries and late times back may be phased out.

Steam specials are usually very popular. The policy of open access has returned steam to some routes for the first time in over twenty years. Well over a hundred different engines (including a few, small, low-powered ones) have worked on the main line since 1971 when *King George V* was permitted to haul the rake of Bulmer's Pullman cars. *Lion,* built in 1838, was 142 years old when it made a number of trips on the main line. Before running on main lines these days a locomotive must pass a series of stringent tests, the most important of which is a steam test on the boiler. If this is successful it results in a boiler certificate being issued. This is valid for seven years after which a major overhaul of the locomotive is required. Insurance companies cover boilers for ten years, so the seven-year period can be extended by three years if certain criteria are met. Before going on main line duty for the first time, or running after overhaul, test runs have to be made, usually at the engine's home base, sometimes followed by a main line trip. In recent years it has become compulsory to have spark arresters fitted, and, in most cases, air brakes. Fit to Run examinations by approved examiners are necessary before each outing. Heritage railways are always happy to service, turn or store locomotives during or between trips.

It is very expensive to maintain locomotives, particularly those for use on principal routes and it is only the hard work of support groups that makes it possible. It cost about £750,000 to totally restore *Flying Scotsman.* The A4 *Union of South Africa* returned to traffic in 2001 after several years, but it is uncertain when the popular A2 *Blue Peter,* managed by the North Eastern Locomotive Preservation Group, will run on the main again because of the cost involved. Even so, in August 2001 no less than 91 steam-hauled trains were scheduled to run.

It should be noted that the numbers and names of a few locomotives are changed from time to time to add variety to the preservation scene, in other words a temporary switch of identity which seems to please a lot of people. *Union of South Africa* ran as *Osprey* for some time when there were anti-apartheid demonstrations. It has also appeared as *Merlin*.

It was quite common to see coaches in as many as five different liveries in one train but the trend now is to have more rakes in the same colour as repainting takes place. Currently there are sets in GW chocolate and cream, SR green, BR maroon or blue and pale grey. Another set is in Oxford blue and cream. More luxurious-looking was the 'Pride of the Nation' train where the shades were those of the former London & North Western Railway – pale blue, blackberry black and gold, but now relivered. A more recent addition is the 'Northern Belle' which supplements the British 'Orient Express' Pullmans. Both of these are owned by the Venice Simplon Orient Express Company (VSOE) but the rest belong to other companies. All this stock is available for hire and travels many miles to fulfil commitments around the country. When rail tours cover three to five days passengers often spend nights in hotels. 'The Royal Scotsman' however is different in that it is a hotel on wheels with its own sleeping cars and special itineraries. Normally the number of passengers is limited to 36, looked after by a staff of about 32. A tour bus shadows the train to take the party on visits to places of interest.

For nine years up to May 2000 there had been an event known as 'Steam on the Met.' in which two sets of mark I or mark II coaches were hauled several times a day by preserved steam locomotives between Watford and Amersham over a three-day period. Up to four engines were used, singly or in pairs. Trade stands from different railway groups were set up on the three station platforms, Rickmansworth being the third one. The locos were stabled at Neasden depot overnight. In the year 2000 they were B12 4-6-0 number 61572 (ex LNER), Ivatt class 2 2-6-2T number 41312 (ex LMS), 94xx 0-6-0 pannier tank 9466 (ex GWR) and K1 2-6-0 62005 also ex LNER. They were supported for 'topping and tailing' purposes by the former Metropolitan Railway electric locomotive number 12 *Sarah Siddons* and a BR class 20 diesel electric, 20227. Six months of planning, mainly in people's spare time, together with commitment by volunteers including London Underground staff, have ensured the success of this popular initiative though its future is in doubt.

For the benefit of steam enthusiasts, goods trains are run at gala events on a good number of heritage lines. The record for the longest freight train in preservation is held by the Great Central Railway, 65 wagons. When Shelton Steelworks in Staffordshire closed in April 2000 after 159 years of production, the occasion was marked by three days of photographic charters. Three 0-4-0 saddle tanks – *Efficient*, *Gasbag* and *Harwarden* (the latter had worked there for 35 years) were taken in by road to star in the event. Other industrial sites have been used but in February 2000 a train of eight 'Dogfish' ballast wagons and a BR brake van were hauled along the Grassington branch in Yorkshire by a standard 4-6-0 number 75014 running as 75019. This was appropriate because '19' was stationed at Skipton at one time. This event cost £9,000 and was only possible because of the willing co-operation of EWS and Railtrack. A year later an 8F 2-8-0 hauled a train of loaded engineers' wagons over the Settle & Carlisle line to mark the completion of a major track renewal programme. It created a scene from the 1960s with a powerful freight engine lugging nearly 800 tons up taxing gradients.

Charter trains on main lines, be they diesel or steam hauled, are always photographed by scores of people. Hearing the chime whistle of an A4 in the distance, then watching it approach, is enough to launch shivers of anticipation – indeed some people have been known to shed a tear of nostalgia . . . then forget to take the photograph!

When do these trains run and who knows the times? This can be summarised as follows:-

>from the itinerary supplied to people travelling on the train
>
>through membership of a railway society
>
>advertisements or tours information in magazines
>
>having a friend 'in the know'
>
>by ringing a number advertised in some magazines
>
>by paying the organisers for timing sheets
>
>from the Internet.

FORMER STAFF

There are retired railwaymen around who have a wealth of knowledge and experience, be they clerks, drivers, guards, porters, p-way men, signalmen, or in any other position. Some are very willing to share their memories and can give a real insight into the people who ran the railways and how their jobs were done – sometimes by expediency rather than the rule book.

Walter, at 102 one of Northumberland's oldest residents, started work as a book lad in a signal box at the age of fourteen. His duties were to record every bell signal in the Train Register Book, carry messages, and generally assist the signalmen. At the same time he gradually learnt all about bell codes, the telegraph, the block system, signals, safety precautions, and how the railways were organised. He became familiar with the Occurrence Book, detonators, single line working, and how to deal with emergencies, before becoming a signalman himself.

Joe, another signalman, recalled how he inadvertently stopped the 'Flying Scotsman' when he was making a cup of tea. When he had pulled off his signals he went to the window and pointed to himself as the express crawled slowly past ("SORRY – my fault!"). The driver held up five accusing fingers, indicating "I have lost five minutes, thanks to you." He then opened the regulator and was away. Joe was glad the driver did not report him, otherwise he would have been asked to explain why he had stopped the train.

Bill, a travelling ticket inspector, told how he had seen a female passenger about to board a train at a busy station tear up her ticket after it had been clipped at the barrier, and throw the pieces on the ground. He kept an eye open for her as he made his way through that train calling, "All tickets, please." When she could not produce her ticket he issued her with a paper 'excess' and made her pay again. She tore that up too, with a "That's what I think of your b—— ticket" remark. The TTI ignored that and continued to check other passengers. He was in a coach near to the exit from the platform when the train pulled in at the lady's destination. He shouted to the porter who would collect the tickets, warning him there was a woman walking along the platform without one. "Make her pay and don't let her pass 'til she does!" She paid three times for her petulance.

There was nothing in BR's rule book which told staff what to do when a barrel of live crabs being unloaded from the brake van of a passenger train was accidentally dropped when the porter caught his finger on a nail in the wood. It caused the hessian covering to burst open and crabs to scuttle all over the platform. There were also no instructions as to what should be done when a prize bull, which had worked its tether loose, charged out of its van when the doors were opened and forced its way into an adjacent field. Common sense prevailed: the staff called in an expert.

Most railway people have a tale to tell. Some, like the above, can be amusing, but these light-hearted episodes do not belittle the real professionalism of true railwaymen. If you do not have contacts with former employees then read articles or books about their experiences. There are a lot of these about now, and they are worth looking up.

INTERNET

Being 'on line' opens the gate to a vast store of information covering every subject imaginable, worldwide. Well over 800 million document pages can be accessed through computer systems linked globally by telecommunications, but this number grows daily at a phenomenal rate. The material is presented in a variety of forms including real-time video with sound, text, charts and graphics.

There are already hundreds of thousands of references to railways, some of which are excellent but others poor. The list includes museums, record offices, libraries and heritage lines. Most study groups have their own Internet site but it is also possible to make in-depth studies of signalling, track, engineering features, accidents – or virtually anything.

The former Railtrack reported on the progress of different schemes and warned of delays or cancellations; Train Operating Companies advertise timetables, special travel offers and future plans. It is also possible to purchase tickets and make seat reservations through the Internet.

Of particular interest to enthusiasts are announcements of special trains and their itineraries. Some people are kind enough to share with others their information of unusual workings, or noteworthy locomotive duties, thereby enabling them to keep a lookout for these or know the progress of charters.

Where subjects are very diverse a few extra words put into the computer will narrow the field. If you asked for information relating to a particular heritage line the response would include such things as houses for sale overlooking that line. By asking, say, for a list of locomotives on that named railway the search is restricted and much time is saved. If the unique worldwide web (www) reference is known this gives quicker access to the site. [Note: such references are not included in this book because there are so many of them, and they do change. Look for them in magazines.] Connecting to 'chat rooms' puts people in touch with others who have similar interests, and information can be exchanged.

Phase One of the Teaching Railway Archives Project (T R A P), for which a Heritage Lottery Funding Application has been submitted, aims to transfer the catalogues of railway archives held at county record offices to the Access to Archives (A2A) Internet web site hosted by the Public Record Office. A second phase aims to produce an on-line guide to all railway-related records in England, Scotland and Wales, concentrating particularly on those archives which are not included in one of the existing on-line cataloguing projects ('Railway Observer').

There can be no doubt that the Internet has already become the premier research tool. Some older people may find it daunting at first but this is the way forward. Even then it will never supersede the feeling of seeing the real thing, be it steam locomotives, rolling stock, or documents prepared so meticulously by real people all those years ago.

LOCAL KNOWLEDGE

Local History Societies and similar groups are flourishing throughout the land. Their members, as a whole, collect and collate information from historical records, documents and plans, tracing the history of their town or village and acquiring photographs to illustrate how life used to be.

Some individuals who have researched their particular interest for a considerable time are happy to speak to their fellow members but there is also an interchange of speakers between societies and others are brought in from outside. Their topics are wide ranging but railway subjects are always popular. These can feature home-made videos, films, slides or audio-visual presentations, even just a talk, but the field is open and the nostalgia flows.

Not everyone wants to join a group or society, preferring to work on their own investigations and assembling their material as a private hobby. Tracing the history of locomotives from a particular manufacturer; or using timetables to work out the longest distance to be covered in the shortest time; or ferreting out track changes over the years at stations on a particular branch are just three illustrations of what can be studied. Inevitably some individual research will be published.

It is quite amazing how quickly word spreads round a neighbourhood when old documents appertaining to railways are discovered in a loft or in a bricked-up wall. Weekly Special Programmes of 1900, ledgers, pocket timetables and Working Timetables relating to the Somerset & Dorset Railway were removed from the walls of a house in Bristol. The loft of a house in Newcastle yielded personal appointment diaries and memorabilia from the 1890s. Godfrey Smith was the District Passenger Superintendent of the North Eastern Railway. An entry dated 26 July 1897 reads,

"North main line to Tweedmouth. Kelso branch to Sprouston . . . from Coldstream to Alnwick, back at 5.30 p.m. 9.35 a.m.-5.30 p.m., at home after." He would travel by an Officers' Special train, known locally as 'the glass carriage'! It was a loft in another part of the country in which were discovered valuable railway posters.

Details of Local History Societies can be found in libraries and some advertise on the Internet.

MAGAZINES

So many people have a love of railways that inevitably there are various publications dedicated to this hobby.

'The Railway Magazine' has been around since 1897 and goes from strength to strength – it even has a 125 power car named after it. Apart from articles on specific subjects, a great deal of information is given in each issue about all types of locomotives and stock relating to new additions, liveries, disposals and transfers. There is news about the latest trains together with progress on preservation projects, all supported by numerous photographs. Like its contemporaries, 'The Railway Magazine' has book and video reviews, answers readers' queries, gives details of forthcoming society meetings or places to visit, and has announcements of special trains. The latter may be followed up in a subsequent issue to show how they performed on the day.

'Steam Railway', as its name suggests, concentrates on heritage lines and steam on the main line. It gives reports on individual locomotives and has carried reports on incognito visits by a reporter to railway centres. It actively supports special appeals for the restoration of locomotives like the ex-Great Central Railway 2-8-0, and spearheaded the scheme to bring together a rake of BR 16-ton mineral wagons to form the 'windcutter' set. Seeing this loose-coupled train with a freight engine at its head, and tailed by a 20-ton brake van is an evocative sight reminiscent of the 1960s. The latest initiative will put *City of Truro* back on the main line in time to celebrate the 100th anniversary of its record breaking run in May 2004.

'Heritage Railways' has news reports from around the country about what is happening on preserved railways. It embraces the various lines as entities, but also gives specific details of steam and diesel locomotives, carriage and wagon news, and the progress of new buildings such as carriage sheds.

'Rail' and 'Modern Railways' are two magazines that present the modern image of track, train operating, and rolling stock companies, among others. They report on new trains, freight traffic, remodelling of stations, the latest in track machines, and the progress of resignalling schemes. In addition, 'Rail' records locomotives class by class, mentioning briefly unusual workings, namings, being commandeered to rescue failed trains, and transfers or disposals. There is news about what is happening around the regions, not forgetting announcements of railtours.

Many railway companies back to pre-Grouping times had their own staff magazines, most of which make fascinating reading. One notable aspect of these publications is the emphasis on peo-ple, not only their work but also their leisure activities including sport.

It is convenient to include in this section publications which are produced in the form of newspapers for railway staff. 'Rail News' is described as "The independent monthly newspaper for people in the rail industry". 'Rail Staff' is promoted as "The industry's select newspaper", whereas 'Track Record' simply stated it was "For the people of Railtrack". All have the common purpose of keeping colleagues informed of what is going on, who is doing what, and what is being done to improve standards. Those who have won awards like the Employee of the Year, or places that have been voted the Best Large Station, are publicised as are safety campaigns relating to trespass and vandalism, even to defying flashing lights at level crossings. Railway staff regularly visit schools in their own time to emphasise the message that railway lines are dangerous places.

As are noted elsewhere, heritage lines and various railway groups produce their own informative in-house magazines.

Souvenirs which have been in families for many years may be passed on to local history groups or private collections in due course. This small memento suggests that two people travelled on this train on 25 August 1937. See also running times in Chapter 14. (Size of original 6" x 4¼")

SEAT PLAN OF "THE SILVER JUBILEE

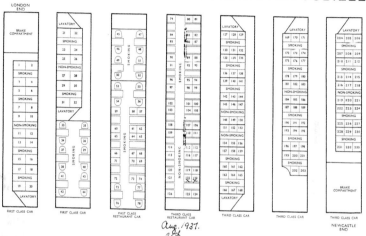

Families and local history groups may have photographs of station staff, like this one taken in 1919, which will include employees in various grades.

ROUTE OF THE
CORONATION
LAND, CRUISE
1953

The following brief notes are given to help the traveller identify the principal points of interest on the route. The tour is divided into four sections—Rhyl to Corwen, Corwen to Barmouth, Barmouth to Afonwen and Afonwen to Rhyl. All references are given looking ahead, that is, facing the direction of travel.

SECTION I—

Rhyl to Corwen

Shortly after leaving Rhyl we cross the Clwyd at its mouth and leave the main line. To the right extends the reclaimed marshland of Morfa Rhuddlan, where, in 796, the Welsh under Caradoc were routed by Offa of Mercia. On our left we pass the village of Rhuddlan, once a considerable port and where, in 1284, Edward I enacted the "Statute of Rhuddlan." The castle, one of four of the strictly concentric type in Wales, was built by Edward I in 1277. St. Asaph, a dignified city-village, is noted as having the smallest cathedral of old foundation in the Kingdom. The next place of interest is Denbigh, a pleasant and important market town, with its castle a conspicuous object to our right as we approach. The castle occupies the site of a British hill-fort and was built in 1284 by Henry Lacy, Earl of Lincoln. From Denbigh we continue through the ever narrowing Vale of Clwyd, with good views of the highest summits of the Clwydian Range to our left, Moel Fammau, with its huge ruin, being especially prominent. The ruin is the remains of the Jubilee Column, erected in 1810 to celebrate the fiftieth year of the reign of George III. Ruthin ("Red Castle") is a quaint little borough standing on a small knoll above the east bank of the river Clwyd, which is here an insignificant stream. In and near the market place are some interesting old timbered houses. The countryside now becomes more wild, and our journey continues through Derwen, shortly after leaving which we part company with the river Clwyd and enter Merioneth. After passing Gwyddelwern, the River Dee is crossed and we arrive at Corwen.

With the Compliments of

BRITISH RAILWAYS

Published material from 1953. (Darlington Railway Centre & Museum)

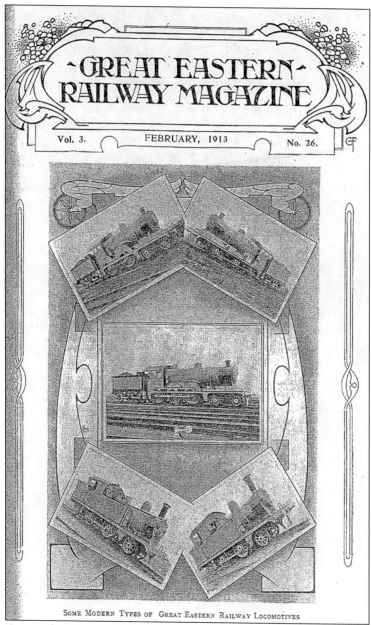

SOME MODERN TYPES OF GREAT EASTERN RAILWAY LOCOMOTIVES

Cover of GER magazine dated February 1913. (National Railway Museum)

Chapter Thirteen
ADDITIONAL SOURCES OF
INFORMATION
(II)
MAPS TO RAILWAY ARCHAEOLOGY

MAPS

When the word 'maps' is mentioned it is logical to think of Ordnance Survey publications, so this is a convenient starting point for what is quite a large subject.

The familiar $1^1/4$ inches to the mile (1:50,000) maps in the Landranger series show the courses of railways, stations including those closed to passengers, tunnels, cuttings, embankments, viaducts, and dismantled railways where track beds and other features still exist. They show how in the early days routes were chosen to take advantage of natural landscapes where practicable, but may also reveal how influential landowners were able to divert railways away from their land. The OS Explorer series is scaled at $2^1/2$ inches to the mile (1:25,000). These maps are useful for helping you to decide where to photograph trains in the environment. Some record offices and libraries have collections in larger scales – 6, 25, and 50 inches, also 10.56 feet per mile. Large-scale maps show defined areas in greater detail, including station buildings and complex track layouts. It is also possible to buy from retailers reprints of old OS maps – say from the 1880s to the early 1900s, when railways were in their heyday. These are ideal sources to show how extensive railway systems were at a port for example.

Maps have been produced to show the proposed, or amended, route for new railways, and the extent of each company's lines at various times in its history. In coal producing areas the various railway companies had maps showing the different collieries and their rail outlets. Some of these maps would mark the limit of railway maintenance.

Railway stations often displayed a framed map of main routes in the British Isles, with ferry connections to and from ports included, but some North Eastern Railway stations, even those of modest size, had tile maps on permanent display showing the extent of their lines. Some of these still survive intact. Perhaps the best example of route maps are those used by London Underground which show every station, interchange points, and connections with the main line stations for the whole system. Their pocket maps are incredible for the amount of detail they have in such a small space. About a century ago Bradshaw's 'Map of the Underground' sold for two (old) pence. Also popular were Bradshaw's Railway Maps of Great Britain, the first of which appeared in 1838.

Worth considering are tourist maps produced by the AA and the RAC. These emphasise roads but railway lines are marked too. Some tourist boards have maps of popular areas like Dartmoor, the Lake District, Snowdonia, and the Borders. These include heritage railways where appropriate, and places to visit. Bartholomew's detailed 'Railway History Map' features the routes of the Big Four, some illustrations of well-known locomotives, notable station buildings, pre-Grouping crests and some historical information. Maps of various kinds are to be found in books and other publications depending on the subject. On a smaller scale are maps in timetables, or the zones covered by runabout tickets.

MODEL RAILWAYS

How can models aid the study of railways? The answer is that the actual objects are recreated in miniature. Today there is a staggering choice of ready-to-run locomotives – steam, diesel and electric – covering the railway eras from pre-Grouping to privatisation, together with coaches and wagons. Kit builders are also well provided for and there are extensive scenic aids available including bridges, trees, passengers, sheep, factories, wagon loads and background scenes.

Railway modelling is such a popular hobby because it embraces making baseboards, planning and laying tracks, electrical work, and creating and building scenery. Above all it encourages observation which in itself leads to research.

Schools which have introduced reasonable-sized model railways (they have been doing so for fifty years at least!) found they helped children in a number of ways:-

ENGLISH Writing about what they have seen or done on the model. Writing for information and letters of thanks.

MATHEMATICS Timing engines round the track with different loads; measuring wagons and coaches, then working out the actual size; what can be bought with different amounts of money; timetables; graphs of hauling capacity of different locomotives.

GEOGRAPHY What the railways carry, shown by appropriate wagons with loads or specific markings; scenic features on the model (cuttings, embankments, tunnels, hills, rivers, etc) to illustrate Ordnance Survey symbols on maps.

HISTORY Railway pioneers; the development of locomotives and passenger travel; signalling from early days to modern times.

ART & CRAFT Groups helping to build the model and scenery, followed by painting and using scatter material. (The children love this!)

SCIENCE Electrical circuits; transformers, the power of steam, electrically-operated points and signals.

These are just a few suggestions which are modified to suit the age of the children. Simple tests are devised to ensure the trains are driven carefully, and on basic (model) railway knowledge. All in all this can be a very useful teaching aid that encourages children to work. A suitable follow-up would be to visit a major station and make a train journey to a railway museum or railway centre.

Individual layouts are as varied as the people who make them. Some enjoy building and testing locomotives, others want to create a motive power depot or branch line. Model railway clubs can usually offer scope for larger layouts, but there is also the exchange of ideas or useful hints from more experienced members. A club may decide to model a terminus with trains arriving and departing, the shunting of stock, and engines moving to and from the depot, following prototype practice. Another possibility is to show a main line and branch at a particular time in their history. The degree of realism that can be achieved is incredible.

Model railway exhibitions, which are widely advertised in magazines, the press, on local radio and TV, and by posters, offer a variety of layouts in different scales, ranging from very simple end-to-end runs to large, complex affairs with a lot of movement. The general public at exhibitions likes to see trains moving and plenty of activity, whereas enthusiasts like to see trains made up and operated in an authentic manner. Parts of the hall are set aside for demonstrations of modelling techniques, also for trade stands and second-hand stalls. Exhibition layouts are taken to different parts of the country by invitation.

Monthly magazines such as the 'Railway Modeller', 'Model Railways' and 'British Railway Modelling' feature layouts, which are well planned and built to a high standard. Model railways can also be viewed at certain museums, heritage railways and commercial premises. All this is a far cry from early tinplate train sets where a clockwork engine would skedaddle along the track and throw itself on its side at the first bend! Even these are sought after by collectors.

NEWSPAPERS

Although bound volumes of newspapers going back many years are held in some newspaper offices and libraries it has been necessary to transfer many of them to microfilms in order to preserve the fragile originals.

Whatever way they are studied, newspapers can give a lot of information about railways, reporting details of meetings, annual reports, the opening of new lines, speed trials, new trains or equipment – things like that. From the beginning of railways, companies advertised the services they offered, together with timetables and notices of excursions. To draw attention to these there would frequently be an illustration of a contemporary locomotive hauling a train of four-wheeled carriages, some with brakesmen standing on the outside. It is easy to assume that the locomotive represented one owned by that particular company, but more usually it was simply a block held by the printer.

Papers gave publicity to staff who had been promoted, or who had retired and been presented with the traditional clock! On the other hand there were reports of people who had been fined, jailed or sentenced to transportation at one time for offences against the railway company or its staff.

For special anniversaries such as the centenary of the Stockton & Darlington Railway some newspapers brought out souvenir issues which are now collectors' items. They have details of the actual events, with numerous illustrations of locomotives, rolling stock, track, buildings, equipment and bridges. The facsimile newspaper dated 3rd July 1925 produced by the 'Northern Echo' makes fascinating reading and includes descriptions of the great procession depicting railways from the beginning to the then modern times. People had come from all over the world to see the "most striking procession of rolling stock ever placed on exhibition". Hundreds of people laid coins on the rails for *Locomotion* to run over. The same newspaper reissued its centenary supplement in 1975 to mark the 150th anniversary of the S & DR.

Newspapers have marked their own centenaries by producing a summary of main events over the hundred years, including of course railways.

Just browsing through old newspapers can often yield more human touches, even though this does not advance railway studies. We may read of an engine crew being attacked on the footplate by owls; or of a pair of would-be thieves who untied part of a tarpaulin covering an open truck and scrambled underneath. The train moved off and travelled for an hour, but movement under the sheet when it stopped alerted a member of staff who quickly tied the cover down and called the police.

Even in modern times reports have appeared in newspapers which are totally inaccurate and misinformed. These are often spotted by readers and sent to magazines like 'Steam Railway'. Three quoted from this source are worthy of note:-

> "Train buffs travelled the length of the country to travel with the Clan Line steam engine built by the Merchant Navy in 1948 at Eastleigh." (*Clan Line* is a Merchant Navy class engine!)
>
> "As railway men know when steam pressure builds up in the boiler, it is dangerous to sit on the safety valve."
>
> "When water was low . . . the quickest and most efficient way of refilling the water was needed. Thousands of gallons of water was pumped into a trough on the edge of the track and when the train rolled in a long pipe was extended from the engine and tipped into the trough. The water was then sucked up into the engine and the journey would continue . . ." (In reality a scoop under the tender was lowered into the trough between the rails and the speed of the moving train forced the water up a pipe into the tender tank. It could also wet people in the leading coach if the window was open.)

Similarly, reports of derailments may be misleading. When a diesel-hauled express left the track one account stated that only the skill of the driver kept the locomotive upright. Things were just as bad, it appears, in 1900 when a heavy roll of matting dropped off a goods train and blocked the adjacent line. A passenger train, we are told, had a miraculous escape when the engine and first three coaches "succeeded in jumping the obstruction".

PHOTOGRAPHS

Think for a moment of the tremendous scope available to railway photographers today:-

> service trains in modern liveries, or a mixture of liveries
> electric or diesel-hauled freight services
> individual locomotives, coaches or wagons
> continental services
> unusual motive power for failures or diversions
> special workings of the Royal Train or touring trains
> trial runs of new stock
> steam charters
> railway architecture
> infrastructure wagons
> railway archaeology

*Trains are often diverted because of engineering operations. This offers enthusiasts more scope to photograph them in unfamiliar surroundings. A1 60143 **Sir Walter Scott** was one train routed away from the main line in August 1960. (Ian S Carr)*

These are just a selection of the themes for which hundreds of films are used every week to produce slides or prints, and now digital images. With some exceptions, similar railway subjects were photographed in BR days, and the post-Grouping and pre-Grouping eras. The result is that thousands and thousands of pictures are now held in libraries, record offices, museums, universities, agencies, and newspaper offices; and by individuals and study groups. In fact photographs are the common factor in all these sources.

Some photographers have made 8" x 6" enlargements available for sale in various outlets. Similarly, some companies have acquired collections and have lists of what is available. There are however, quite a large number of individuals who are happy to allow copies of their work to be sold to help organisations like heritage railways, locomotive preservation groups and restoration projects.

The question of copyright is often misunderstood or even ignored. Fees can be charged if permission is given for photographs to be reproduced in books or publications. From 1998 the copyright duration for photographs was extended to *50 years after the death of the person who took the photographs.* Prior to that it was 50 years after the first public display or publication thereof.

PLANS

It is a sobering thought that drawings have been prepared for almost every item that has ever been constructed for our railways.

Designs for locomotives vary from outline diagrams with basic dimensions to highly detailed plans and elevations. Each part, including the arrangement of controls in the cab, is also drawn out separately. Passenger coaches show not only the external features but also include the interior layout and refinements. Drawings of wagons incorporate styles of wheels, buffers, brakes and special requirements bearing in mind the loads they are to carry. The amount of detail shown on drawings largely depends on who will be using the plans.

Buildings naturally include stations as a whole, waiting rooms, signal boxes, goods sheds and cattle docks. Alterations such as a new bathroom in the station master's house, a proposed platform extension, or a renewed water supply (among other things) all demand detailed planning by architects and engineers.

Track diagrams, sometimes produced on what are known as white prints, show the layout of stations, goods yards, engine sheds, sidings and depots. They may indicate the numbers of points and signals corresponding to those on levers in the signal box. Many show the length of each section of track and sometimes how many standard size wagons they can hold. Any planned alterations are noted, or indicated by dotted lines, so that it is possible to see at a glance what difference will be made once the work is completed. The Railway Clearing House used to publish diagrams of stations and junctions which showed track layouts in different colours to identify which sections belonged to the various pre-Grouping companies.

Diagrams are prepared for other diverse reasons such as loading and transporting an out-of-gauge load, stabling the Royal Train, or to accompany an official Accident Report.

It is not only railway employees who are, or were, engaged to provide plans, a large number have been supplied by private firms as part of the tendering procedure.

Hundreds of prints showing programmes, proposals or intentions are available for reference in principal libraries, record offices, museums and railway centres, or by joining a railway group. In due course many more will be available on the Internet to supplement what is already there. It is possible to acquire copies or originals when a collector is disposing of unwanted items at auctions, exhibitions, or privately.

PUBLISHED MATERIAL & PAPERWORK

Visit any library or bookshop and you will see an array of railway books, in fact so many have been published over the years that virtually every aspect of railways, ancient and modern, has been covered. These are books written *about* railways but there is another category that consists of books or booklets mainly *for* the railway industry. It is a selection of these that should be considered, as fewer people are aware of them.

Most pre-Grouping railway companies published their own Rule Book but those that did not would adapt one from another company by arrangement. From the earliest days the emphasis was on safety, that is the protection of passengers, staff and railway property. A typical instruction circa 1860 would state, "When any train or engine has stopped at a station, or passes a station without stopping, the danger signal must be exhibited immediately and shall remain so until the train or engine shall have left the station five minutes [or whatever]. The signal is then made to indicate that all is right." Signals by lamps were:-

Red, a signal of danger. STOP.
Green, a signal of caution. PROCEED SLOWLY.
White, a signal of all right. GO ON.

Later, for safety reasons, yellow was used for caution and green for all clear, the reason being that more 'white' lights were appearing beside railway lines and it was confusing for drivers. Passenger trains had to be given priority over mineral, goods or livestock traffic.

On the Blyth & Tyne Railway in Northumberland, a passenger who could not – or would not – produce a ticket when asked by a member of staff could be detained and, if absolutely necessary, "be conveyed before a magistrate with as little delay as possible". Luggage could be retained to offset an unpaid fare.

A guard on the Midland Railway pre-1900 had to be in attendance half an hour before his train was due to start. The train itself was under the control of the guard and it was he who passed instructions to the driver. He had to be satisfied before and during the journey that the train was properly loaded, marshalled, coupled, lamped, greased and sheeted where necessary, also that the brakes were working correctly.

Railway companies issued instruction booklets to staff about (among other things) the correct loading of wagons, how loads were to be secured to prevent them from moving in transit, and how to open truck doors to prevent injury. It was a good policy to keep your feet out of the way before letting the side door of an open truck drop onto the loading platform! Firemen were warned not to climb on top of the tender while the engine was moving, especially if there were gantries or overbridges. Similarly, anyone in a carriage needing to open a door and climb down onto the ballast was urged to open the window and look out first to check there was no-one outside who could be injured, if not scalped, by the door.

Today, companies distribute literature regarding electric trains, hazardous loads, modern equipment . . . and protection when working on the track, particularly near electrified rails or overhead wires. The Personalised Rule Book issued by Railtrack was more than 1$\frac{1}{2}$ inches thick. Other modern documents which might be found are detailed specifications regarding the different examinations and servicing levels for locomotives, multiple units and rolling stock. In the era of Privatisation, documents are published by companies that seek to compete for a franchise or to extend or renew one they currently hold.

'Published Material' is an extremely broad field covering many years of railway operation and it includes advertising by manu-

facturers and the railways themselves. What to look for on particular journeys, holidays, special wagons available for particular
loads, and the services available to industry are just some of the
topics. As early as 1923 (the year of the Grouping) the Great
Western Railway published a 130-page soft-backed book called
'The 10-30 Limited'. Described as "A Railway Book for Boys of all
Ages", it gave many details of the 'Cornish Riviera Express' and
of railways in general. Within a few months 71,000 copies had
been sold. It was quickly followed by 'Caerphilly Castle – a Book
of Railway Locomotives for Boys of all Ages', at the price of one
shilling. A 150-piece jigsaw of this locomotive was on sale at the
British Empire Exhibition for two shillings and sixpence, or by
post 3/- (i.e. 15p).

It was about 1933 that the first 'Railway Handbook' appeared
from the Railway Publishing Company. It deserves a special mention as it was designed to provide students of railways with a collection of statistics and a wide selection of other information. The
96 pages of the 1939-40 booklet cover many diverse topics and are
packed with facts. British Rail used to publish a neat little booklet
for staff with the title 'Facts & Figures about British Railways'.

Look for miscellaneous published material of this kind in the
usual places previously mentioned. Early examples and those
from pre-Nationalisation days are not so easily obtained at sales
of various kinds, but it is worth keeping a look out for them.
Perhaps auction sales give the best chances of acquiring what is
generally known as 'paper work'. For convenience, lots are
made up of bundles or boxes of papers and documents, so it can
be something of a lucky bag.

Most of these documents were never intended for publication
nor indeed for preservation, they were simply methods of transferring information from one place to another, usually a central
point where statistics could be compiled. How many tickets
were issued at a particular station and how much money was
taken; how many head of cattle were despatched, or how many
tons of coal were conveyed, and how did the figures compare
with the same period in previous years; which engines at a particular depot were available for work on a given day, and how
many locos of each class were there . . . this kind of data appeals
to people who are interested in the practical details of railway
working. Paperwork is an invaluable source of information
which can open avenues of further research.

RAILWAY ARCHAEOLOGY

For the purpose of this book, railway archaeology is defined as railway items from a bygone age, still in use though not necessarily for their original function, or still to be seen in their former place but no longer used.

It can be said that every station has its own history, some more interesting or extensive than others, but many of them were built when buildings of distinction reflected the prominence of railway companies. The entrance to London's Waterloo shows grandeur and stateliness. St Pancras was built as a gothic masterpiece, elegant and majestic, because the Midland Railway wanted to create a building that would be the envy of the world. Manchester Victoria today combines the dignity of the old with the practicality of the new. The verandah along the front still shows on the ironwork the destinations of some travellers – Blackpool, Belgium, Goole, Ireland, Scotland . . . a reminder of the station's importance in the past. Inside, near the old booking hall, is a huge wall map of the Lancashire & Yorkshire Railway. Adjacent to the stairs that led to a toilet is a frosted glass window engraved

Evidence of railway archaeology can be found in various places. This stone reads:-

GELT BRIDGE
Francis Giles Civil Engineer
John McKay Builder
MDCCCXXXII   MDCCCXXXV
(1832-1835)

(J A Wells)

Initials of railway companies can be found in a variety of places. Ironwork for canopies was one favoured place, in this case LNER. (J A Wells)

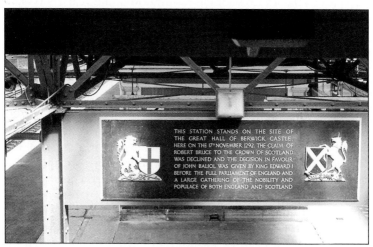

THIS STATION STANDS ON THE SITE OF THE GREAT HALL OF BERWICK CASTLE. HERE ON THE 17ᵗʰ NOVEMBER 1292, THE CLAIM OF ROBERT BRUCE TO THE CROWN OF SCOTLAND WAS DECLINED AND THE DECISION IN FAVOUR OF JOHN BALIOL WAS GIVEN BY KING EDWARD I BEFORE THE FULL PARLIAMENT OF ENGLAND AND A LARGE GATHERING OF THE NOBILITY AND POPULACE OF BOTH ENGLAND AND SCOTLAND

Passengers descending the steps leading to the platforms at Berwick cannot fail to see this notice giving historical information. (J A Wells)

'Gentlemens Lavatory'. Nearby is the smart RESTAURANT sign of long ago, and below it is printed the modern image BAR together with "eat Quick Snack fresh" – contrasting styles of the ornate and the functional. At Glasgow Central 6.8 acres of glass roof, covering an area three times the size of the old Wembley stadium,

This water tank at Haltwhistle in Northumberland was built for the Newcastle & Carlisle Railway. It was still standing in 2002. (J A Wells)

was part of the award-winning restoration in the year 2000 of all the Victorian stone and glasswork. 200 period light fittings were installed, a good example of reintroducing ideas from our heritage. In the early 1960s the lavish Victorian buffet at Newcastle was 'modernised'; now, thankfully, it has been restored to its former glory. These reminders of the past are there for all to see, and there are hundreds like them, but we need to look a little more closely at what are forgotten details.

Company initials or names can still be seen in stations and on buildings. Baker Street Underground shows evidence of the Metropolitan Railway. Elsewhere, awnings, seats, plaques and notices may still have indications of previous ownership. The North Eastern railway even stamped NER on nail heads, but probably to deter theft. The station at Berwick-upon-Tweed has a notice on the footbridge stating that it was built on the site of the great hall of Berwick Castle. Dates can also be spotted on buildings or viaducts. The former water tank with the lamp room beneath at Haltwhistle shows it was constructed by R. Wylie & Co. of Newcastle in 1861 for the Newcastle & Carlisle Railway.

Because of closures, numerous buildings were sold off or rented out and are now used for different purposes. Stations have been converted into very desirable residences, used for shops, as Scout premises, or for commercial activities such as post offices and council offices. Goods sheds have become garages for road vehicles; workshops, or stores for furniture and equipment. Some signal boxes have been converted into weekend cottages, even a burger bar. Former engine sheds have been turned into a variety of businesses depending on their size. They are now factories, council depots, timber yards, used on farms, and for wagon works, scrap yards, even a potato store. One depot in Northampton, the former London & North Western Railway shed from 1881, is used by the Civil Engineers' Department.

Redundant coaches serve as cricket pavilions, hotel and restaurant extensions or weekend homes. On heritage lines they can

Redundant railway vans can be found in a variety of premises where their sturdy construction makes ideal storage areas. Vans on farms may also be used to house animals or birds. (J A Wells)

provide accommodation for volunteers, or be let as holiday bases. Old covered vans may be seen in sidings where they are used as storage areas, but grounded bodies also appear in builders' yards, on factory sites, and on farms where they can provide a home for pigs or poultry. Former coal drops at country stations are known to have been roofed over and have doors fitted on the front to make substantial sheds. Old fish-belly rails from former waggonways have turned up during ploughing, and some have been found supporting the roof of lead mines in Cumbria.

You can come across examples of railway archaeology in unexpected places; it is worth keeping a lookout and if you are not sure about something, then ask.

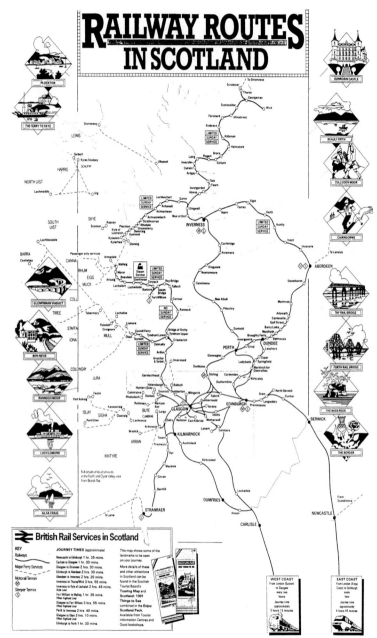

A Scottish Tourist Board touring map of 1984.

GOODS TRAFFIC.

NUMBER OF TONS	CARTED Local	Foreign	Total	NOT CARTED Other than Cheeses A and B — Local	Foreign	Total	NOT CARTED Cheeses A and B — Local	Foreign	Total	TOTAL Local	Foreign	Total
Forwarded	3530	1131	4661	9771	619	10390	1736	121	1859	15034	1371	16410
Received	7267	5544	15531	32667	1226	37013	15643	1564	17224	55619	14254	70073
Total	10817	9675	20492	42655	47454	47403	17363	1705	19058	70353	16125	86643

Goods Traffic Nett Debit ... £ 21981 - 13.

LIVE STOCK TRAFFIC.

NUMBER	Horses in Trucks	Cattle	Calves	Sheep	Pigs	Geese	Number of Wagons of Live Stock — Local	Foreign
Forwarded	39	203	-	216	3	-	71	2
Received	128	3137	66	3929	1722	40	604	9
Total	167	3340	66	4145	1725	40	675	11

Live Stock Traffic Nett Debit ... £ 421 . 11.

GOODS SPECIAL DEBITS.

Description and Amount (State any not shewn)					
Cartage by Horse ...	461	14	2	Haulage ...	4 3
" " Motor				Haulage Transfer Charges ...	14 6
Timber Loading ...	96	15	9	Wharfage	
Sack Charges				Labourage...	14 0
Wagon and Sheet De-				Special Wagon Charges	
murrage ...	12	0	0	Wagon Hire ...	2 2 11
Storage and Warehouse				Wagon Tolls ...	17 9 0
Rent ...	7	7	1	Sheet Hire ...	2 10 0
Weighing (in Carts) ...	1	9	6	SHUNTING	
" (in Wagons) ...	2	2	6	Split Deliveries ...	12 0
				Sawdust ...	10 0
				Insurance	
				Yard Rent...	1 16 6
				Siding Rent	
				Cranage ...	1
				Grain Samples ...	9

Total Goods Special Debits ... £ 6/13 10

Total Debit Goods Department (as per Account Current) £

Paperwork: An example of goods traffic handled at one station in the year ended 31st December 1908.

This diagram of part of Tweedmouth shows main through lines (dotted), reception roads and sidings for goods traffic, a fairly large motive power depot, and lines serving works and the docks. There was also a special bench where cattle wagons were cleaned and disinfected after use. Diagrams like this were used for years at a time and indicated alterations, or when lines were removed, hence many have shown signs of frequent use. Apart from the main tracks, 184 locations are identified on the original.

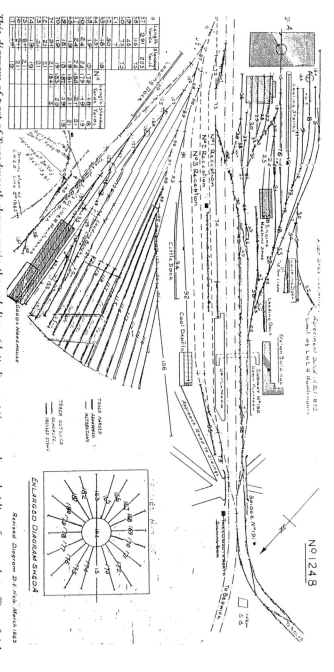

ENLARGED DIAGRAM SHED A

Revised Diagram D.E.H.Cle. March 1943

N° 1248

20-TON PLATE WAGON (FITTED WITH FIXED TRESTLE). E 14

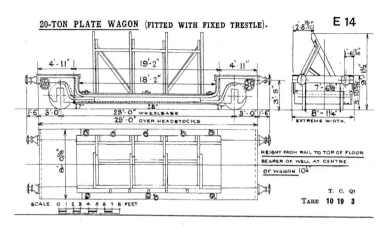

20-TON PULLEY WAGON. E 15

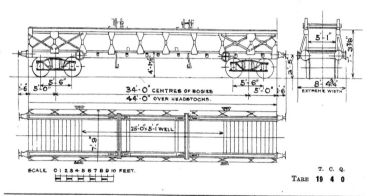

40-TON PLATE WAGON (FITTED WITH FIXED TRESTLE). E 16

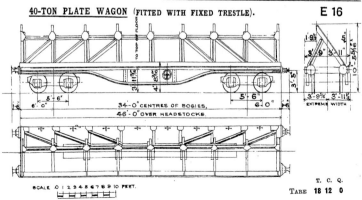

Plans of three specially constructed wagons, 1917.

Here is a table which will enable you readily to ascertain the speed of trains in miles per hour by taking the time occupied in seconds in travelling between any two consecutive quarter-mile posts.

Time in seconds between quarter-mile posts	Speed of train— Miles per hour	Time in seconds between quarter-mile posts	Speed of train— Miles per hour
10	90	21	42·8
11	81·81	22	40·9
12	75	23	39·11
13	69·2	24	37·5
14	64·28	25	36
15	60	26	34·6
16	56·2	27	33·3
17	52·9	28	32·1
18	50	29	31
19	47·4	30	30
20	45		

NOTE : *Nine hundred, divided by the number of seconds occupied by a train travelling between any two quarter-mile posts, will give you the speed of the train in miles per hour.*

An extract from 'The 10.30 Limited' published by the Great Western Railway in 1923.

Chapter Fourteen
ADDITIONAL SOURCES OF INFORMATION
(III)
RAILWAY ART TO VIDEOS
RAILWAY ART

It is extremely difficult to portray a steam locomotive accurately to get the perspective and proportion just right. Those who have this gift produce some striking paintings; but there are some individuals whose work is used on public house signs or greeting cards that are best ignored.

Older readers may recall the carriage prints by C Hamilton Ellis which were framed beneath the luggage racks in some passenger coaches. He depicted railway scenes under the title Travel in . . . (and gave the year). 1835 illustrates the 0-4-2 Leicester & Swannington Railway's engine *Samson:* "the first locomotive in the world to be fitted with a whistle, then called a steam trumpet". It was hauling a half-open coach and one totally open to the elements. 1845 shows a 2-2-0 London & Birmingham Railway, number 32, hauling an express which includes a Royal Mail van. The engine has no protection for the crew, but an extra detail is the driver waving to a lady in a crinoline dress and bonnet, and her soldier companion, on the other side of the fence. Travel in 1905 depicts the new Midland Railway 4-4-0 compound locomotive number 1000 speeding along with bogie coaches.

David Shepherd is a household name for his impressive illustrations of African wild life, particularly elephants. His locomotive paintings are equally full of spirit and character.

David Western created large images which have been on show in exhibitions at the National Railway Museum and elsewhere. His displays have included detailed colliery scenes with very early locomotives; a Stirling single on shed, oozing atmosphere; and composite pictures based on Sir Nigel Gresley and Sir William Stanier and their creations.

Terence Cuneo, one of the most versatile of artists, has illustrated forceful railway scenes that unquestionably capture his subject. From his originals copies were made for display on railway billboards. His trademark is a mouse which is included in every picture – running along the track, sitting on a locomotive, disguised as an insulator on a telegraph pole, or just watching the trains go by. The original painting of *Flying Scotsman* on the Forth Bridge sold for £26,000 in 1996.

The Guild of Railway Artists has some extremely talented members whose work is shown in annual exhibitions, notably at York.

A selection from the paintings by C. Hamilton Ellis which really capture the spirit of railways. They all have a wealth of historical detail. The originals and copyright are held by the National Railway Museum.

RAILWAY SOCIETIES

Railway Correspondence & Travel Society

The Railway Correspondence & Travel Society has roots going back to 1927 when a handful of enthusiasts met in a garden shed and formed the Cheltenham Spa Railway Society. The name was changed within weeks to its present title and the membership is now about 4,000, scattered around the world. Branch meetings are held regularly in 27 places in the UK and visits are arranged to works, depots and other places of interest.

The Society's magazine 'The Railway Observer', which has been published every month since 1932, carries news from all over the rail system, supplemented by photographs.

The RCTS launched its first publication in 1935. It was the 'Locomotive Stock Book', a comprehensive list of the locos at work in Great Britain, and was very successful. Many books of engine histories have been produced since then, enjoying a reputation for accuracy and authenticity. They cover classes of the Big Four and British Railways.

This Society has amassed a huge collection of 3,000 books and pamphlets, historical records, and about 1,500 bound volumes and magazines. Surplus books, magazines and post cards are available for sale to members from its library in Uxbridge. Each year branches organise stands at engineering exhibitions, model railway events and railway open days. The RCTS is highly regarded by enthusiasts and railway employees.

North Eastern Railway Association

As its name suggests, the North Eastern Railway Association caters for all those who are interested in the NER, including the Hull & Barnsley Railway and other companies which had become part of the North Eastern, together with its successors.

Formed in 1961, the Association has grown to more than 600 members whose diverse interests cover locomotives, rolling stock, stations and other buildings, signalling, road vehicles owned by the company, shipping, timetables, and general operations. There are active groups which hold indoor meetings and outdoor activities in areas associated with the North Eastern Railway, like York, and Hull; also in London for those living further south.

Members benefit from the exchange of information with others who have similar interests and may have carried out detailed research on diverse subjects ranging from breakdown trains to snowploughs and signal boxes. The Association has an extensive library of books, historical drawings and documents, plans and photographs, all of which are held at Darlington Railway Centre. Members, including modellers, find these resources invaluable. A high quality, illustrated magazine, the 'North Eastern Express', is published each quarter together with newsletters and supplements to disseminate information to members. So far there have been more than 150 issues, all comprehensively indexed. The Association has also published some excellent, highly detailed and profusely illustrated books, most notable of which are the three volumes of 'North Eastern Record'. These were produced jointly with the Historical Model Railway Society (q.v.).

Narrow Gauge Railway Society
The Narrow Gauge Railway Society was founded in 1951 to stimulate interest in all forms of narrow gauge rail transport and now has a membership of over 1,400 worldwide. Members' interests cover every aspect of construction, operation, history and modelling. The Society has built up a wealth of archive material and a sizeable library over the years. It owns two locomotives, *Townsend Hook* and *Peter*, but has been involved in preserving others, together with rolling stock. The Society's magazine 'Narrow Gauge News' is published six times a year.

Industrial Railway Society
Similarly, the Industrial Railway Society, which was formed in 1937, aims to record the fullest possible information about this category of locomotive together with the business history of companies that have operated industrial railway systems. This group maintains a very high standard of research and has a very good collection of books and other material (much of it unpublished), also photographs. The Society preserved an Aveling & Porter locomotive from Beckton Gas Works which is now housed in the Transport Museum at Covent Garden. Members also saved a Kerr Stuart loco named *Pixie* but this is now owned by the Leighton Buzzard Narrow Gauge Railway.

The Midland Railway Society
The Midland Railway was incorporated in May 1844 by the amalgamation of the North Midland, Midland Counties, and the Birmingham & Derby Junction railways, making it one of the most influential of the pre-Grouping railways. Its locomotives and rolling stock were some of the best in the country.

The Midland Railway Society seeks to bring together those who are interested in the Midland Railway including its predecessors, and successors, lines operated jointly with other companies, and its working practices. The Society publishes a historical journal three times a year and four newsletters. Meetings are held regularly and visits are made to places of interest, relating especially to the Midland Railway and the LMS. Members' interests cover architecture and civil engineering, the historical aspect, locomotives, carriages, wagons, signalling, traffic returns, paper work and rail tickets.

Historical Model Railway Society

The Historical Model Railway Society has for the past 50 years gathered, stored, exchanged and distributed railway information to historians, modellers and enthusiasts. It is recognised as one of the principal sources of accurate information about railways from the earliest days to the present time. It has an ever-expanding collection of drawings and photos. Already over 30,000 negatives have been transferred to 'PhotoCAT', the Society's computer.

The HMRS – which is a registered charity – has established an Award Fund to encourage young people up to 25 years of age, who are in full-time or part-time education, to become actively involved in research into our railway heritage. This can be purely academic, or to gather information with the aim if constructing an historically accurate model railway. Cash awards are available to individuals, groups, schools and colleges. The scheme is complementary to the national curriculum.

The Society's 'Collectors' Corner' provides a method for researchers and collectors of railway models to exchange information.

Institution of Mechanical Engineers

Founded by 'The Father of Railways' – George Stephenson himself – the Institution of Mechanical Engineers is a professional body with about 83,000 members throughout the world. Of these, some 5,000 are associated with the railway industry in various forms. Think of steam locomotives, the interlocking of points and signals, bridges, high-speed trains and modern track laying machines, and you have a bird's eye view of *some* of the work of railway engineers over a long period of time. Today technology demands an entirely new range of skills but the Institution has a tradition of making things happen and adapting to a changing world.

This organisation aims to be the leading forum for the exchange of knowledge and expertise. It publishes a number of magazines, journals and volumes of technical information. Booklets and video programmes are also available.

Southern Electric Group

The Southern Railway, formed as one of the Big Four in 1923, developed an intricate system of routes in south east England using London Waterloo as the hub of operations. It favoured an intensive service of electric multiple units feeding from an elevated third (or 'live') rail. A number of devotees of these trains, some of them interested in the modelling aspect, formed the Southern Electric Group in 1970 to study and record past operations, the then current scene (no pun intended!) and on-going development. It is now recognised as the leading organisation in its field.

The Group runs a Sussex Branch and a South Hampshire Branch, both of which have monthly meetings offering talks, slide shows and other attractions.

A bi-monthly magazine, appropriately called 'Live Rail', includes articles and features, together with rolling stock updates and reports on the introduction of new stock for faster services since Privatisation. The group publishes books relating to Southern electrics, which are also available to non-members.

Unusual in preservation, the Southern Electric group owns the only main line electric multiple unit train in the United Kingdom. It is a '4Cor' set, number 3142, built in 1938 for the electrification to Portsmouth and Bognor Regis. Currently under restoration by volunteers, it is kept at St Leonard's in East Sussex. It is hoped to return the set to operational use for charter work.

The above are just a representative selection of railway societies.

REPLICA LOCOMOTIVES

It is one thing to see an ancient steam locomotive like *Locomotion* or *Rocket* in a museum but it is a totally different experience to see it in working order, showing particularly how it was constructed and how it operated. For obvious reasons it is not feasible to run the originals but thanks to the construction of replicas these things are now possible. This has been done very successfully with both of these famous engines, and others. Thanks to modern technology in the form of virtual reality, scenes like the opening of the Stockton & Darlington Railway in 1825 can be recreated.

The new *Locomotion* is based at Beamish, the North of England Open Air Museum, in County Durham. Hauling a replica open coach and a chaldron waggon, it made 7,500 trips along the Museum's Pockerley Waggonway during the summer season of the year 2000, and covered 3,000 miles. It worked 203 days out of 204. Beamish has completed the £330,000 construction of an 1815 0-6-0 locomotive called *Elephant*. A painting from circa 1820 was used as a basis for the design, the original of which was a Blenkinsopp style rack engine. The next project is to recreate *Puffing Billy*.

*Chaldron waggons continued to be used in colliery yards until the 1950s. The chaldron weighed up to 2¹/₂ tons and carried 2 tons 13 cwts of coal. The replica of **Locomotion** stands at the head of four waggons at Beamish Open Air Museum in County Durham. (David A Wells)*

A replica of Richard Trevithick's locomotive of 1802 was completed in 1990 for the Ironbridge Gorge Museum. At the end of 2001 it was in the National Railway Museum. The Trevithick Society intends to build a copy of the pioneer's steam driven road carriage, forerunner of his railway locomotive.

The original *Sans Pareil* built by Timothy Hackworth did not win the Rainhill Trials but it was a successful locomotive of the time and worked on the Stockton & Darlington Railway. The replica, built in 1980, is based at the Timothy Hackworth Museum at Shildon but it does visit heritage lines for special occasions. Unfortunately, during one of these relocations the engine and tender were damaged in a low-speed derailment and the replica open coach was written off.

George Stephenson's *Planet* was a 2-2-0 built in 1830 for the Liverpool & Manchester Railway. Features of its design were the outside sandwich frames and inside cylinders in the bottom of the smokebox, the first of its type. It was the Museum of Science & Industry at Manchester that built the imitation.

As mentioned elsewhere, a broad gauge 2-2-2, *Fire Fly* is under construction at Didcot. A standard gauge 2-2-2 'bloomer' was being built by the former Birmingham Railway Museum but the project is on hold because of other commitments. The museum's name has now been changed to Tyseley Locomotive Works & Vintage Trains.

The line between a replica and a total rebuild can be a narrow one. In 1860 Sharp Stewart of Manchester supplied an 0-4-0 tender engine to the Furness Railway at a cost of £9,641/4/2. It was converted to a saddle tank and worked for nearly a century in that form. It was rebuilt in 1999 to its original style as number 20, with a four-wheeled tender, by the Lakeside & Haverthwaite Railway in the Lake District. This red locomotive, on its third visit away from its home, was used to inaugurate a new platform and an extra demonstration line at Barrow Hill Engine Shed.

The Great Western Railway 150 event in 1985 included a replica of *Iron Duke,* built by the Science Museum. It ran on the short section of broad gauge track at Didcot and on a demonstration length laid in Kensington Gardens, London. It is now at York, together with a broad gauge coach.

An exception to the statement at the beginning of this section is a locomotive which could easily be taken for a look-alike but is actually the original. The Liverpool & Manchester Railway's 0-4-2 *Lion* was totally restored for an event to mark the 150th anniversary of the railway in 1980. It had played an important role in the film 'The Titfield Thunderbolt' in 1952.

STAFF RECORDS

These days the majority of staff records are held at the Public Record Office, Kew, though some remain in county record offices and elsewhere. These will include transcripts or photocopies of originals. These records are of particular interest to those engaged in family history research or to people who are curious about jobs or grades that are obsolete on the modern railway.

There are dozens of categories, lists, registers, ledgers, applications and the like, and the following are just a hint at the scope available:-

Names and grades of staff employed at particular stations
Cleaners and firemen recommended for promotion
Fines / suspensions / dismissals for misdeeds
Service history of individuals
Sack Superintendent's office staff (Great Eastern Railway)
Office boys and messengers
Survey of weekly household budget of senior clerks (NER)
Carting, stable and market staff (Midland Railway)
Roll of Honour of staff who joined HM forces, 1914-1915
Register of booking constables, etc. (Lancashire & Yorks. R.)

These headings are abstracted from 'Was Your Grandfather a Railwayman?' by Tom Richards – a very detailed directory of railway archive sources.

Staff records exist from the earliest days of railways but inevitably there are huge gaps. Nevertheless we should be thankful that so many have survived but it takes time and patience to research this subject.

SMITH, Arthur   April 13th 1877

DATE	STATION	EMPLOYMENT	WAGE per week
Jan. 16th 1893	Darlington South Jct.	Ass't. Signalman	8/-
Feb. 10th 1894	-ditto-	-ditto-	9/-
Oct. 20th 1894	-ditto-	-ditto-	10/-
May 4th 1895	-ditto-	-ditto-	12/-
Feb. 25th 1897	Darlington	Lad parcels porter	... (not shown)
Mar. 3rd 1897	-ditto-	Lamp lighter	9/-
Aug. 28th 1897	Darlington North Road	-ditto-	11/-
Oct. 16th 1897	Darlington Park Gate	Signal lad	11/-
Aug. 20th 1898	-ditto-	-ditto-	13/-
Aug. 19th 1899	-ditto-	-ditto-	15/-
Sept. 23rd 1899	Darlington South Jct.	Ass't. Signalman	18/-
Jan. 1st 1900	-ditto-	-ditto-	19/-
Feb. 7th 1900	R 6/6 L 6/6	Colour Good (*eye test*)	
Mar. 2nd 1900	Barras	5th Signalman	24/6
May 19th 1900	Barras Summit	Signalman	25/-
July 20th 1901	West Hartlepool	Relief Porter	24/-
		Block knowledge	1/-
July 19th 1902	-ditto-	Relief Porter	25/-
		Block knowledge	1/-
Aug. 6th 1905	Hesleden	Signalman	24/6
Nov. 17th 1906	-ditto-	-ditto-	25/-
Apr. 18th 1911	R 6/9 L 6/9 B 6/6	(V normal)	
June 22nd 1912	Hesleden	Signalman	26/-
Jan. 3rd 1914	-ditto-	-ditto-	27/-
Oct. 11th 1915	Wingate	-ditto-	27/-
Dec. 13th 1916	Thornaby	-ditto-	27/-

(Remainder of service not recorded in this document)

HISTORY
March 7ᵗʰ 1896   Enlisted as a soldier, case entered on Dismissed Servants
Return for May. Reinstated during strike, Feb. 25ᵗʰ 1897 as Parcels Porter at
Darlington.
Jan. 30ᵗʰ/07   Omitted to lower signal for 6-17pm pass'r train W H'pool to
Ferryhill causing delay of 2 minutes.
First Aid 1ˢᵗ Exam June '06 Hesleden.
Nov.1/'07   Caused 9 mins delay to the 10-38am Pass'r train S'dland (i.e.
Sunderland) to West H'pool by allowing a Mineral train to leave Hesleden
Bank Head with too small a margin.
First Aid 2ⁿᵈ Exam June 1907 Hesleden.
-ditto- Final Exam July 1908 -ditto-.   Medallion No. 118949.
Oct. 30ᵗʰ/09   Overlooked excursion in programme and let Mineral out in front
of it on Oct 23ʳᵈ. Had to be set back and delayed excursion 5 minutes.
Nov. 3/1910   Overlooked excursion in Programme & allowed Mineral train to
draw out of sidings causing 9 mins delay to the Excursion on Oct 22ⁿᵈ.
Cautioned and told if a similar case occurs in future he will be more severely
dealt with.
Jan. 25ᵗʰ 1913.   Slept in & came on duty 40 minutes late on Jan. 13ᵗʰ 1913.
Dec. 24/13.   Slept in and box not opened until 6-30 instead of 5-30 am as
instructed. Mineral train delayed 25 mins in consequence.

(Staff record. Darlington Railway Centre and Museum)

Staff magazines from railway companies and BR survive in certain libraries, railway centres and record offices, and are another useful source of records. Changes of job, promotions, sport, competition results, good ideas, retirements and obituaries are included. Some magazines arranged visits to meet staff at the stations where they worked and published photographs of them individually or in a group.

The current 'Rail News' mentions staff by name who have achieved awards, prevented accidents, or who are in the news. A 'What's On' section lists meetings and activities of railway groups.

TELEVISION & RADIO

Over a long period of time many excellent programmes have been broadcast or shown on television, covering aspects of railway history, rail journeys and railway holidays. These are repeated from time to time and it is worth watching out for them.

TIMETABLES

The name of Bradshaw is synonymous with railway timetables. Original railway companies issued their own times of trains and many gave connecting services with other companies, but in 1839 George Bradshaw (already known for his reproduction of maps from 1827) produced a book containing timetables of northern railways. He subsequently covered the whole of Great Britain and Ireland, but it was at the end of 1841 that he first published a monthly volume to take account of train alterations or additions. These were known as 'Bradshaw's General Railway & Steam Navigation Guides' and continued under his name until the early 1960s. Long before that however these very popular books were simply called 'A Bradshaw' because they were so well known. By 1910 the number of pages was 1,000.

These guides not only gave train times, they also included the distance of each station from the trains' departure points, connections, and the routes, supplemented by maps. All were indexed and cross-referenced. Considerable advertising was included particularly for hotels and private schools, plus numerous brief but eye-catching lines boldly printed at the bottom of pages.

Libraries, museums, record offices and railway centres often have collections of timetables covering many years. Whether these are national, regional or local, comprehensive or in leaflet form, railway researchers are given an insight into the sort of service that operated from their local station, or elsewhere, at a given time. This is particularly useful where stations or whole sections of line have been closed. Some people consult old timetables to find out how long it would have taken them to travel from A to B via C, or to work out how many miles they could cover on a rover ticket.

Timetables for staff are different from those for the public. These are the Working Time Tables – WTTs for short – but in some places in pre-Grouping days they were called Service Timetables. As they evolved they became more complex by sometimes embracing what the trains conveyed, their classification, specific working instructions, speed restrictions, and crew times, apart from departure, passing and arrival times.

The National Railway Museum has in its archives a table of goods trains run by the London & Birmingham Railway in 1846; also an 1852 WTT, divided into passenger and goods sections, for the use of Company Servants only. The freight section specified the names of collieries whose coal each train was permitted to convey. This may have been a special, exclusive arrangement. Some railway companies demanded that WTTs were destroyed as soon as they were replaced by new issues.

TOURIST OFFICES

Tourist offices are regularly sent supplies of leaflets advertising places to visit and things to see. For people interested in railways there will be information available about heritage lines in the area, even further afield. Museums too will be represented and there may even be a miniature or narrow gauge railway in the grounds of a stately home. Some tourist offices have a selection of books for sale which might include railways in different parts of the country.

VIDEOS

In the 1950s and 60s the British Transport Commission Film Unit produced some excellent 16mm films, first in black and white then in colour. Some of these featured places of interest in selected towns and cities but included footage about the railway itself. Other films presented specific topics such as the 'Elizabethan Express', 'Night Mail', and 'Snow Drift at Bleath Gill' in which huge drifts were charged by a steam powered snowplough train in an attempt to rescue a stranded goods train. The effects were spectacular. These films could be borrowed by schools and various groups provided they were returned in good condition and on time.

The film unit crew had access to locations all over the system not normally available to members of the public. Nevertheless, at the same time, numerous individuals filmed trains in 16mm from station platforms and from bridges, roads or fields near railway tracks. Even more people used 8mm size film to record the railway scene. Both professional and amateur films have been included in video programmes, giving us invaluable memories of steam. The three films mentioned above are available as Film Classics, and we should not forget the reissue on video of popular films like 'Oh! Mr. Porter', 'The Titfield Thunderbolt' and 'The Railway Children' (original version).

The number of videos featuring railways continues to grow rapidly, so what sort of subjects do they cover? Preserved steam locomotives on main line charters are produced year on year, sometimes in two parts. These show engines at rest, going to pick up their train, pulling out of stations, working hard on gradients and travelling at their maximum permitted speed. Steam power in general, from forty or fifty years or so ago, is a feature of some videos; others show steam on particular routes like north of Newcastle, or the Somerset & Dorset, or steam in defined areas which include Shropshire, Wales and Scotland. Of particular interest to some enthusiasts are videos which unveil steam centres as they used to be. A whole tape may be devoted to one class of locomotive working in different locations, like the

9F, class 37 or 47 diesels and the new class 66s. There are programmes devoted to *Flying Scotsman* because of its fame.

Trains diverted from their normal routes may involve electric locomotives being hauled by diesels where there is no electrification; or freightliner traffic passing along unusual lines. Cab Rides give a driver's eye view from, say, a TransPennine express, or from London to York, or from a class 56 on freight duty. The overview of freight traffic in different parts of the country is another topic regularly included.

Videos are also produced for heritage railways such as the North Yorkshire Moors, the Severn Valley and the Kent & East Sussex. It is an opportunity to show off their locomotives and stock and the attractive scenery through which their particular line runs. These are a good substitute when it is not possible to make a personal visit to a preserved line; on the other hand they can be viewed before a proposed visit to ensure you know what to look for.

For those interested in railways abroad there are numerous productions covering all five continents.

Railway magazines regularly carry advertisements for videos which can be obtained by mail order, through the Internet and over the counter from shops including those that deal in model railways. They can also be bought at model exhibitions, swap-meets, car boot sales, market stalls and second hand shops. The quality of previously used tapes cannot be guaranteed.

Numerous people today own video cameras and enjoy making their own compilations. Whatever way you use them, it is another way of extending your railway knowledge.

'THE SILVER JUBILEE" RUNNING TIMES

MONDAYS TO FRIDAYS EXCEPT ON JUNE 3RD AND 6TH JULY 29TH, AUGUST 1ST, 1938

Distance from Newcastle Mls. Chns.	Station		Time a.m.	Point to Point Time Mins.	Distance Mls. Chns.	Speed Miles per hour
	Newcastle (C.)	dep.	10. 0			
5 39	Birtley	pass	10. 8	8	5 39	41·2
14 3	Durham	pass	10.18	10	8 44	51·3
23 18	Ferryhill	pass	10.28	10	9 15	55·1
36 6	Darlington	arr.	10.40	12	12 68	64·2
	Darlington	dep.	10.42			
50 20	Northallerton	pass	10.55	13	14 14	65·4
58 —	Thirsk	pass	11. 1	8	7 60	77·5
69 2	Alne	pass	11. 9	8	11 2	82·6
80 16	York	pass	11.19	10	11 14	67·0
94 2	Selby	pass	11.33	14	13 66	59·3
112 30	Doncaster (C.)	pass	11.49	16	18 28	68·8
			a.m.			
129 57½	Retford	pass	12. 5	15	17 27½	69·4
148 18½	Newark	pass	12.20	15	18 41	69·4
162 70¾	Grantham	pass	12.32	12	14 51¼	73·2
191 78½	Peterborough (N.)	pass	12.55½	23½	29 7½	74·3
209 37½	Huntingdon (N.)	pass	1.11½	16	17 39½	65·6
236 33¾	Hitchin	pass	1.32½	21	26 76	77·0
250 68½	Hatfield	pass	1.44½	11½	14 19½	74·3
268 27	King's Cross	arr.	2. 0	16½	17 54	66·3

Average speed between Darlington and King's Cross, 70.4

Over-all speed, 67.08 miles per hour

CONNECTING SERVICES TO LONDON

VIA NEWCASTLE

		a.m.
Alnmouth	dep.	8.44
Blyth	,,	8.43
Carlisle	,,	8.10
Haltwhistle	,,	8.46
Hexham	,,	9.16
Monkseaton	,,	9.17
Whitley Bay	,,	9.19
Tynemouth	,,	9.24
South Shields	,,	9.10
Sunderland	,,	9.30

VIA DARLINGTON

		a.m.
Durham	dep.	9.54
West Hartlepool	,,	9.35
Stockton	,,	10.0
Saltburn	,,	9.12
Redcar	,,	9.19
Middlesbrough	,,	10.0

"THE CORONATION" LEAVES KING'S CROSS MONDAYS TO FRIDAYS 4.0 P.M. DUE NEWCASTLE (CENTRAL) 7.57 P.M.; AND NEWCASTLE (CENTRAL) MONDAYS TO FRIDAYS AT 6.31 P.M. DUE KING'S CROSS 10.30 P.M.

MONDAYS TO FRIDAYS EXCEPT ON JUNE 3RD AND 6TH JULY 29TH, AUGUST 1ST, 1938

Distance from King's Cross Mls. Chns.	Station		Time p.m.	Point to Point Time Mins.	Distance Mls. Chns.	Speed Miles per hour
	King's Cross	dep.	5.30			
17 54½	Hatfield	pass	5.49½	19½	17 54½	54·4
31 73½	Hitchin	pass	6. 0½	11	13 19¼	77·7
58 69½	Peterborough (N.)	pass	6.19½	19	26 76	85·1
76 29	Huntingdon (N.)	pass	6.34½	15	17 39½	70·0
105 36½	Grantham	pass	6.59	24½	29 7½	71·2
120 8½	Newark	pass	7.11	12	14 51¼	72·2
138 49½	Retford	pass	7.26	15	18 41	73·2
155 77	Doncaster (C.)	pass	7.40½	14½	17 27½	72·0
174 25	Selby	pass	7.56	15½	18 28	71·0
188 11	York	pass	8. 8	12	13 66	70·0
199 25	Alne	pass	8.20	12	11 14	56·7
210 27	Thirsk	pass	8.29	9	11 2	73·5
218 7	Northallerton	pass	8.35	6	7 60	77·5
232 21	Darlington	arr.	8.48	13	14 14	65·4
		dep.	8.50			
245 9	Ferryhill	pass	9.15	12	12 58	59·3
254 24	Durham	pass	9.23	8	9 15	45·9
262 68	Birtley	pass	9.23	8	8 44	64·1
268 27	Newcastle (C.)	arr.	9.30	7	5 39	47·0

Average speed between King's Cross and Darlington, 70.4

Overall-speed, 67.08 miles per hour

CONNECTING SERVICES FROM LONDON

VIA DARLINGTON

		p.m.
Middlesbrough	arr.	9.27
Redcar	,,	9.52
Saltburn	,,	10.7
Stockton	,,	9.32
West Hartlepool	,,	9.55
Durham	,,	9.45

VIA NEWCASTLE

		p.m.
Sunderland	arr.	10.17
South Shields	,,	10. 7
Tynemouth	,,	10.14
Whitley Bay	,,	10.10
Monkseaton	,,	10. 8
Hexham	,,	10.30
Haltwhistle	,,	11.32
Carlisle	,,	11.38
Blyth	,,	10.49
Alnmouth	,,	10.49

"THE CORONATION" LEAVES KING'S CROSS MONDAYS TO FRIDAYS 4.0 P.M. DUE NEWCASTLE (CENTRAL) 7.57 P.M.; AND NEWCASTLE (CENTRAL) MONDAYS TO FRIDAYS AT 6.31 P.M. DUE KING'S CROSS 10.30 P.M.

Three days before hauling the inaugural 'Silver Jubilee' service, number 2509 Silver Link twice reached a speed of 112 mph.

In general, working timetables (WTTs) for the use of staff covered main lines and branches on particular routes. Sometimes it was more convenient to have pages for a much more limited area, as for example between Tweedmouth and Berwick, which were just over a mile apart near the Scottish border. These show regular, timetabled trains, but there were numerous others such as mineral traffic, light engine movements and additional trains that were not timetabled, only slotted in.

Extract from a working timetable. October 1934-April 1935.

EXPLANATION OF REFERENCES

B	Extra allowance to recover delays.	ⅡC	Single Line Section; no token provided.	ThX	Thursdays excepted.
C	Collect tickets.			ThO	Thursdays only.
D	Stops only to set down (Passenger or Goods).	✢	Staff Station.	FX	Fridays excepted.
		⊕	Electric Staff or Tablet Station.	FO	Fridays only.
E	Examine tickets.			SX	Saturdays excepted.
G	Runs via Goods Lines.	✚	No. 2 Express Goods (Braked)	SO	Saturdays only.

B — Extra allowance to recover delays.
C — Collect tickets.
D — Stops only to set down (Passenger or Goods).
E — Examine tickets.
G — Runs via Goods Lines.
L — Stops only for locomotive purposes.
N — Does not attach or detach.
R — Allowance for Refreshments or Lavatory purposes.
T — Through line.
U — Stops only to take up or attach (Passenger or Goods)
W — Stops only for engine to take water.
DD — Stops only to set down and detach (Passenger or Goods)
EP — Express Passenger Train.
HC — Horse boxes and carriage trucks are not conveyed by this train.
OP — Stopping Passenger Train.

ⅡC — Single Line Section; no token provided.
✢ — Staff Station.
⊕ — Electric Staff or Tablet Station.
✚ — No. 2 Express Goods (Braked)
▲ — No. 2 Express Goods (Unbraked)
* — Stops when required (Passenger or Goods).
† — Empty train.
§ — Light Engine.
— — Stands for other trains to pass.
** — Stops when required for specific purposes (*see footnote*).
Q — Runs when required.
MX — Mondays excepted.
MO — Mondays only.
TX — Tuesdays excepted.
TO — Tuesdays only.
WX — Wednesdays excepted.
WO — Wednesdays only.

ThX — Thursdays excepted.
ThO — Thursdays only.
FX — Fridays excepted.
FO — Fridays only.
SX — Saturdays excepted.
SO — Saturdays only.
MTO — Mondays and Tuesdays only. Similar explanations apply to **MWO, TWO**, &c.
MTX — Mondays and Tuesdays excepted. Similar explanations apply to **MWX, TWX**, &c.
MOQ — Mondays only, but not unless required. Similar explanations apply to **TOQ, WOQ**. &c.
MXQ — Mondays excepted, runs only when required on other days. Similar explanations apply to **TXQ, WXQ**, &c.
Alt MO — Alternate Mondays only. Similar explanations apply to **Alt TO, Alt WO**, &c.

The above references are also used in Programmes and other working notices.

The general information and special instructions for the guidance of station masters, engine drivers, guards, and others in reference to the working of the line, are contained in the appendix to the Working Time Table Book.

This appendix is issued from time to time, as circumstances may render necessary, and each station master, engine driver, guard, and other servant of the Company supplied with working books must take care to have a copy of the latest issue in his possession.

C. M. JENKIN JONES *Superintendent*

(Darlington Railway Centre and Museum)

PART THREE
THE CHOICE IS YOURS

Chapter Fifteen
LOCOMOTIVES

This is the most popular of topics relating to railways, dating perhaps from when the main ambition of many young boys was to be an engine driver – someone controlling a huge, powerful machine, travelling at high speed, the envy of numerous admirers of the iron horse! As it is a vast subject it may be difficult to know where to begin. Things have moved on since the days of steam, so why not start with modern traction? Read about today's locomotives in magazines and books, watch videos, and talk to people until parts of the jigsaw slot into place. Gradually extend your knowledge to include steam engines and at some time your inclination will be to make a more in-depth study of particular subjects and to delve into their history. The suggestions which follow are not in any order of merit as it is for individuals to choose what pleases them most.

You may wish to look at the work of locomotive superintendents whose influence on designs has produced some wonderful locomotives of impeccable workmanship and detail. Whole books have been written about these people and to mention a few by name in no way decries the achievements of so many other locomotive engineers. William Adams had a flair for 4-4-2 tank engines, but he also produced efficient 4-4-0 express types for the London & South Western Railway until he was 73. They were noted for their smooth riding and steady running particularly when entering curves, thanks largely to the long wheelbase of the leading bogie.

Patrick Stirling took charge of the Great Northern locomotive fleet in 1866 and four years later launched for express work the stylish 4-2-2 engines with massive driving wheels eight feet in diameter. They were aristocratic greyhounds once they 'got going', a combination of grace and harmony.

George Jackson Churchward, who had been chief assistant to William Dean of the Great Western Railway, made major contributions to the design of famous engines like *City of Truro*. One of these was the flat-topped Belpair firebox for greater efficiency. When 'GJC' himself became loco superintendent this became a standard feature of Great Western engines, together with distinctive domeless, tapered boilers, a brass casing for the safety valves, and copper-capped chimneys. Wilson Worsdell succeeded his brother, Thomas William Worsdell, as 'loco super' of the North Eastern Railway. He produced a series of vary reliable and aesthetic locomotives that offered good protection for crews. His M class 4-4-0 achieved distinction in the Railway Races of 1895, and his smart 4-6-0 design was the first with this arrangement for passenger work. The P3 (LNER/BR J27), first built in 1906, worked through to the end of steam, and one of the class, 65894, is still active. It is to revert to North Eastern Railway number 2392. The following information is one example of what can be extracted from notes about a particular locomotive class. The original sheet had locomotives listed in numerical order.

ALLOCATION OF L.N.E.R. LOCOMOTIVES AS AT 11 JAN.1947
(Extracts)
· CLASS J 27

SHED	LOCOMOTIVES ALLOCATED					
Alnmouth	5889	5892				
Borough Gardens	5817	5846				
Haverton Hill	5787	5806	5818	5830	5853	5855
	5859	5866				
Heaton	5781	5794	5795	5824	5826	5842
	5862	5863	5864	5886	5893	
Neville Hill	5861	5883	5885	5888	5894	
Normanton	5782					
North Blyth	5783	5786	5789	5797	5799	5801
	5804	5811	5819	5828	5851	5876
	5877	5879	5880			
Percy Main	5780	5784	5791	5792	5796	5802
	5809	5812	5813	5814	5815	5821
	5822	5825	5831	5837	5838	5839
	5852	5858				
Selby	5827	5836	5844	5845	5848	5849
	5874	5875	5881	5882	5890	5891
South Blyth	5808	5810	5829	5834		
Stockton	5788	5800	5805	5807	5857	5860
	5865	5867	5870	5887		
Sunderland	5785	5793	5798	5820	5823	5833
	5835	5840	5843	5847	5854	5856
	5872	5878	5884			
Tweedmouth	5869	5873				
West Hartlepool	5790	5803	5816	5832	5841	5850
	5868	5871				

[K Hoole collection   Darlington Railway Centre & Museum]

Locomotive superintendents changed companies when they sought a different challenge, so they would take their own ideas with them when they moved on. Similarly, employees of more junior rank who were promoted to chief would incorporate into their future designs some of the features they had seen introduced and probably shared in. In this way the inspiration of the head of the company would spread to others.

Another aspect of study could be to select a particular wheel arrangement and compare the different styles owned by one company, or more than one. How many 4-4-0 and 0-6-0 tender engines were built? Why were some successful and others not? Why did some look right and others lack harmony? What made an engine stand out and be noted against others? Was it size, performance, elegance, livery, or what?

Thinking beyond the output of railway company works, you may want to look more closely at private firms which have built locomotives for home and overseas for many years. If construction is not your scene what about a survey of engines housed at various depots at different periods? The shed could belong to one company only or be situated in a particular area. Some would prefer to study rosters that govern each working day. These are designed to make the best use of available motive power as cheaply as possible. Two examples from the days of steam will serve as illustrations.

Passenger Engine Working Commencing 17/9/1956 – DERBY
Turn 1 One class 6P/5F (ex LMS) 4-6-0

		Derby	Dep.	1-20am	Pass.	MO
Arr.	1-51am	Nottingham		2-30	ES	MO
	2-33	Nottingham CS				
		Derby		3-57	Pcls.	MX
	4-37	Nottingham			LE	MX
		Nottingham CS		7-15	ES	Daily
	7-18	Nottingham		7-35	Pass.	D
	8-9	Derby		8-15	Pass.	D
	11-58am	Bristol TM				
		Bristol TM		4-45pm	Pass.	D
	8-15pm	Derby				

This tells us that on Mondays only the locomotive was scheduled to take a passenger train from Derby at 1-20am to Nottingham then take the empty stock to the nearby carriage sidings.

On other days it left Derby at 3-57am to take a parcels train to Nottingham after which it ran light engine to the carriage sidings and brought empty stock back into the station. It left Nottingham at 7-35, including Mondays, with a passenger train to Derby where it arrived at 8-9am then left six minutes later for Bristol Temple Meads. The return trip left there at 4-45 for Derby. [Note – the engine would have to be kept coaled, watered and oiled ready for its next duty.]

Turn 3 One class 6P/5F (ex LMS) 4-6-0 (Amended)

		Chaddeston	Dep. 6-52am	ES	MO
Arr.	7-2am	Derby	–		
		Park Sidings	7-5	ES	MX
	7-22	Derby	–		
		Derby	8-5	Pass.	SX
	10-45	St Pancras	12-25pm	LE	SX
	12-31	Kentish Town shed			
		Derby	7-55am	Pass.	SO
	10-39	St Pancras			
		Kentish Town shed	4-58pm	LE	D
	5-8	St Pancras	5-30	Pass.	D
	8-47	Nottingham	8-55	ES	D
	8-58	Nottingham CS	11-20	ES	D
	11-23	Nottingham	11-55	Pass.	
	12-31	Derby		ES	MX and Sun.
	12-46	Park Sidings			

The amended No 3 turn used the same class of engine, a Jubilee. On Mondays only the allotted locomotive brought empty stock from Chaddeston to Derby, arriving at 7-2am. On other days the empty coaches came from Park Sidings. It then hauled a passenger train to London St Pancras, arriving 10-45. On Saturdays the train left Derby ten minutes earlier at 7-55am, arriving St. Pancras at 10-39. The loco was on shed at Kentish Town until 4-58 when it ran light engine (LE, i.e. on its own) to the terminus and left at 5-30pm for Nottingham (arr. 8-47). The empty stock was taken to the carriage sidings for servicing prior to the 11-55pm departure from Nottingham to Derby and from there to the carriage sidings.

[Extracts from Passenger Engine Workings, Winter 1956/57
National Railway Museum Library]

*Formerly named **Bihar & Orissa**, Jubilee class 4-6-0 number 45581 heads a parcels train to Manchester in July 1966. The shed plate, 55C, shows the engine was based at Farnley Junction. (Ian S Carr)*

Performances of locomotives of many kinds on main line runs have been well documented over many years, recording projected and actual times, route, load, speeds, distances, signal checks, speed restrictions, weather conditions, and often the names of the crew. Different classes may be compared over the same run, or the same type of locomotive may be logged on different days. These statistics are also compiled for preserved steam engines working modern charters. Back in time it was quite a common occurrence to use the dynamometer car to give accurate readings of an engine's capabilities on the track. These records are usually filed away or are in magazines. You may, on the other hand, want to start your own timings as a different hobby.

Reference has been made elsewhere in this book to liveries, another fascinating subject whatever the locomotive. Class 47 diesels have been around for a long time. They have been painted green, blue, grey, red, and a combination of colours at different times. When the diversity of details are considered – like the size and positioning of numbers and corporate signs, or how far the yellow front wraps round the cab – the number of variations runs into dozens.

If you want to see the largest collection of genuine locomotive nameplates, the best place to visit is the National Railway

Museum where numerous examples are on display, not forgetting those still on the locomotives themselves. The most usual places for names to be shown are on the side of the smokebox or above one of the splashers. Diesels and electric locomotives have their names on the body side. The list for subjects for names is extensive to say the least. Apart from those mentioned elsewhere there are towns and cities, mountains, cathedrals, racehorses, manors, personalities, regiments, lochs, and birds, to name a few. When Rail Express Systems, a parcels and mail service, was introduced it was decided to name the diesel locomotives by using words beginning with RES – thus we had *Restored* and *Respected* among them. Anyone unfamiliar with the reason could conclude that here was an engine that had been restored, or wonder why the other should be respected! When they ran out of suitable names they switched to saints. When it realised money could be made BR was happy to use names commercially. It is still a subject of interest all the same.

Engine crews in particular frequently gave locomotives a nickname which quickly stuck to the class. McConnell of the London & North Western Railway designed a 2-2-2 engine with a six-wheeled tender, painted a rich vermilion and with brass fittings. Not all the driving wheels were covered by the splasher, quickly earning the class the name of 'Bloomers'. At that time an American lady, Mrs Amelia Bloomer, was urging women to wear short, full skirts and bloomers. Originally these were short, loose trousers gathered at the knee. The LNER/BR V1s or V3s were 'teddy bears'; a certain design of LMS 2-6-0s were 'crabs', 2-4-2 tank engines were called 'double-enders', and the air-smoothed Southern types were given the name of 'Spamcans'. ('Spam' was the trade name of tinned meat made mainly from pork, during World War II.) Some railway enthusiasts have taken to giving nicknames to modern traction, so we have 'growlers' (class 37), 'gridirons' (class 56), 'wardrobes' (class 58) and numerous others.

For those more interested in the people who drove or fired the trains, staff records from motive power depots can bring the human touch. Notice the sections on eyesight tests, a very important qualification for those seeking to be firemen or drivers. On the Midland Railway at one time long ago a staff of wood nine inches long and two inches wide, excluding the handle, was used. (➤ page 176)

N.E.R. Loco. Department.   REGISTER OF ENGINEMEN & FIREMEN

John Butterley

DATE	RATE	STATION	DATE	SUNDRY EVENTS
Jan. 20 1883	3/-	Tyne Dock	Feby. 22 1864	Born
July 3 1883	3/4		Jany. 20 1883	Entered Co's Service
Feby. 7 1889	3/8			as Fireman.
Aug. 8 1889	4/-		Jany. 20 1883	Appointed as Fireman
Nov. 29 1889	4/3		## Dec. 12 1893	Appointed as Driver.
Feby. 6 1890	4/9			
Dec. 12 1893	5/6		## Aug. 3 1894	Promoted to Driver &
Aug. 16 1894	6/-			ante-dated to Dec. 12/93.
Oct. 13 1899	6/6			
Jany. 1 1900	7/-		Feby. 27 1928	Left the Service.
Dec. 12 1900	7/6			Cause of leaving :- Ill-health S 231.
Aug. 18 1919	15/-			

EYESIGHT TESTS

		Colour	Form		
			R	L	B
Jany.	5 1894	Good	6/6	6/6	6/6
Jany.	15 1904	Good	6/6	6/6	6/6
May	3 1910	Normal	6/6	6/9	6/6
May	19 1915	Normal	6/36	6/36	6/36
June	1 1915	Tested at Pilmoor			
June	13 1916	-ditto-			
June	7 1917	-ditto-			
Aug.	1 1923	Normal	6/36	6/36	6/36
Oct.	30 1923	Tested at Pilmoor			
Oct.	23 1925	-ditto-			
Nov.	4 1925	Normal	6/60	6/60	6/60
		Hypermetropic			

Name   John Butterley   7/1602

DATE	AMOUNT	PARTICULARS OF FINES & REPRIMANDS (Black) OF REWARDS AND COMMENDATIONS (Red)
Sept. 7 1901	Cautioned	Having Van off at a pair of points at Ebchester, Eng. 744, Aug. 10.
Nov. 7 1903	-ditto-	Coming late on duty Oct. 27.
June 11 1904	-ditto-	Having van off the line and bending drawbar of Engine 1982 at No. 4 Hole, Tyne Dock, Apl 27.
Feb. 2 1907	-ditto-	Not reporting to Operative Dept. that engine 1984 was unfit for 2nd shift of work, Jan 4/07.
Dec. 7 to 14 1912	*£3-6-0*	*Loyal during strike.*
March 3 1917	St. Caution	Causing a collision between Engine 1939 and 317 Feb 10/1917.
Mar. 27 1920	Reprimand	Taking wood from a wagon, but as there was an element of doubt he was given benefit of it. Feb 19/1920.
Aug. 9 1924	Susp 2 days	Passing shunting signal at danger, Wagon Shops Sdgs. Tyne Dk. Eng 290 drl (derailed) 22/7/24.
Mch 16 1927	Fined 5/-	Not observing that the regulator of one of the Engines was open resulting in a collision between light Engines and Wooden Erections At Long Shed, Tyne Dock, Jany 10/1927. G1/733.

EXTRACT FROM RECORDS OF THOMAS BELL

Date of birth   8th April 1870:
Entered Company's service as Cleaner   15th October 1885
Appointed fireman   28th August 1890
Appointed driver   14th July 1899

Name   Thomas Bell   15/94

DATE	AMOUNT	PARTICULARS OF FINES & REPRIMANDS (Black) OF REWARDS AND COMMENDATIONS (RED)
Oct. 4 1890	2 - 6	Having engine 106 off rails at Tyne Dock and not reporting same, Sept. 12.
July 25 1891	Cautioned	Coming late on duty, July 20.
Sept. 29 1894	-ditto-	- ditto- Sept. 11.
Dec. 22 1894	1 - 6	-ditto-
Jan. 19 1895	3 - 0	Absent from duty, Jan. 2.
Aug. 24 1895	Strong caution	-ditto- Aug. 6.
Nov. 16 1895	5 - 0	Coming late on duty, Oct. 31.
Dec. 14 1895	Strong caution & warned.	Absent from duty Nov. 6 & 11.
May 16 1896	5 - 0	Absent from duty, Apl. 30.
Aug. 15 1896	Suspended 1 week.	–ditto- Aug. 4.
Nov. 20 1897	Strong Caution	-ditto- Nov. 15.
Jan. 1 1898	Suspended 2 weeks	-ditto- Dec. 21.
June 18 1898	5 - 0	Coming late on duty, May 23 & 26.
Oct. 29 1898	Note	Absent from duty, saying he was ill, Oct 24.
Mar. 17 1900	Cautioned	Coming late on duty, Mar. 5.
Apl. 14 1900	-ditto-	Absent from duty, Mar.19.
June 16 1900	-ditto-	Having engine 290 off at a pair of points at No.3 Bank, Tyne Dock, Apl. 13.
Sept. 15 1900	-ditto-	Absent from duty, Sept. 4.
Feb. 16 1901	3 - 0	-ditto- Jany. 29
Apl. 20 1901	5 - 0	Coming late on duty, Apl. 6.
Oct. 3 1903	Cautioned	Absent from duty, Sept. 18.
July 9 1904	-ditto-	-ditto- June 25.
Aug. 6 1904	2 - 6	Causing Engines 1993 & 2001 to be derailed at New Shed Road, Tyne Dock, June 13.
Jan. 14 1905	Caution	Absent from duty Dec. 27.
Feb. 18 1905	3 - 0	-ditto- Jan. 28.
Jan. 4 1908	Caution	Coming late on duty, Dec. 17/07.
Apl. 11 1908	Strong Caution	-ditto- Apl. 1/08.
June 19 1909	Caution	-ditto- June 7/09.
Feb. 25 1911	-ditto-	Not satisfying himself that he had received proper signal before setting back, result 2 wagons derailed at Stanhope Sdgs, Tyne Dock, Jan. 24/1911.
Jan. 20 1912	Dismissed	Being under the influence of drink, Dec. 23/1911.

[Staff Record   Darlington Railway Centre & Museum]

L 3175   1/8417—5000—30/3/22   S37/253

NORTH EASTERN RAILWAY.

LOCO. DEPT.,

York .... 192...

History of ......Aaron Bell Convey,   4/24,   Driver,   Heaton.

PROMOTIONS.

Date of Birth ....Jan. 7/1878	**Fireman**...............................
Entd. Co's Service....May..1/1899........	
Com. to Fire....Dec. 12/1899	**Driver** ....Dec. 19/1922
	15/-
Com. to Drive....Oct. 21/1918	
ante dated 19/12/1917.	
Eyesight Test....Oct. 3/1923	**Colour**....Normal............. **Form** $6/_6$ $6/_9$ $6/_6$

Date.		How dealt with.	Particulars of Fines, etc.
Oct. 23	1905	Caution	Losing time through having engine 444 short of steam with 5-40pm Heaton to Berwick, and 9-45pm Tweedmouth to Heaton.
Jan. 8	1906	Fined 1/-	Late on duty.
Aug. 17	1908	Caution	Absent from duty
Aug. 19	1909	do	Late on duty.
Aug. 1	1910	Susp. 1 day	Not keeping a proper look-out and running engine 1817 into tender of engine 1908, result tender of engine 1817 was derailed, also causing damage to tenders of both engines and Per.Way at Gateshead.
Dec.7-14	1912	£1-10-0	ON STRIKE.
Nov. 8.	1915	Note	Personally warned by Mr Baister for not preparing engine properly and when spoken to by Driver J.W.Halford, he commenced to swear and threaten Halford.
June 29	1922	Susp.1 day	Whilst in charge of 1138 and after receiving a caution signal at Norwood Jct. Cabin to run to caution to Dunston East, not being prepared to stop clear of anything in the section resulting in a collision with a Mineral Van.
Dec.25	1925	Caution	Stopping at Smeafield in error.
Dec. 12	1926	St.Caution	Stopping in error at Ferryhill when working 6-43pm E.P.York to Newcastle.
Dec. 12	1926	Susp. 1 day	Passing signal at danger, Alne, when working 1-50pm Newcastle to York, Engine 2209.
July 12	'927	Fined 2/6	Causing collision between Engines 1918 x 1187 at Coal Stage - Heaton -

On each white surface were three sets of black squares, 1/4 x 1/4 inch. The candidate had to be able to count from a distance of fifteen feet the number of dots in any group selected by the examiner. For the men who may have been colour-blind, or 'colour ignorant', the wool test was used. Up to 40 pieces of coloured wool in all shades were hung on a stand in a row and had to be identified. Bits of wool representing the colours of danger and caution had also to be matched with those on the stand. A driver whose sight was beginning to fail would be transferred to shunting duties or taken off driving altogether.

Chapter Sixteen
PASSENGER SERVICES AND FREIGHT
PASSENGER TRAFFIC

In the previous chapter it was suggested that a study of locomotives could start with modern traction before exploring other aspects. The same could be said of passenger traffic. Make yourself familiar with 125s, 225s, loco-hauled expresses, Eurostars, diesel and electric multiple units, and new trains on London Underground. Use magazines, books and videos to help you assimilate the basic background. You can then begin to look more thoroughly at mark I stock on heritage railways and experience what travel was like in the 1950s, bearing in mind the slow crawl on these lines cannot equate to full main line use. There are of course charters running on various routes where speeds up to 75mph are acceptable – but the days of mark I coaches on main lines are numbered, on the instructions of the Health & Safety Executive.

Some lines have beautifully restored four-wheeled and six-wheeled stock from Victorian days. If these are an inspiration to you then fill the gaps by reading up about the historical development of rail travel since the first few, faltering turns of the wheels that led to moving people around over greater distances. Be original by seeing if you can unearth something that other researchers have missed. Look into major museums and see for yourself the coach builders' craft, and that of painters.

What else is on offer for this aspect of railways? You can look at named expresses, their departure points, routes, destinations and timings. Headboard and carriage roof boards can be included. The workings of Royal Trains, and their composition, are worth investigating. What about the evolution of electric trains; the methods of lighting trains, brakes, couplings, and safety measures?

There were the inter-connecting Royal Mail trains covering the whole country at one time, which can be compared with the current Railnet system. In the study of railways one aspect leads to another.

At one time railway companies had locomotives on stand-by at various places along a main route in case an engine should 'fail' during its journey. In this way a train could resume its trip as quickly as possible. Today rescue diesel locomotives, nicknamed

'Thunderbirds', have to cover much larger areas and it may take two or three hours to reach a stranded train. In the same way there used to be spare sets in carriage sidings which could be brought into use when required. Now, every train is used extensively, though they do have to be serviced. '225' trains, usually hauled by class 91 electric locomotives, work from King's Cross to Leeds, or to Glasgow via Newcastle and Edinburgh. For destinations further north, notably Aberdeen and Inverness, the older 125s are used, but there are only a few of these sets. In either case, if any of these trains is delayed or has to be withdrawn for any reason, the knock-on effect is enormous, causing late running and cancellations over a wide area. The same applies to the whole rail network.

This brings us to another subject which many people find absorbing – carriage working. This is normally a complex arrangement to have trains in the right place at the right time, and (hopefully) with sufficient accommodation. Planners who worked out how to integrate new Virgin CrossCountry services into the national network spent three years in complex negotiations "involving eighteen train operators, seven Railtrack zones, five Passenger Transport Executives, two freight companies, 120 local councils, and a large number of Passenger Councils" (Virgin Trains). From October 2002 it was planned to have 230 Virgin Voyager trains into and out of Birmingham New Street a day, thereby doubling the number of weekly timetable services.

By contrast we shall consider the working of the 9-25am express from Glasgow on its journey as far as York on Saturdays 8th July to 2nd September 1939. This is shown in the diagram taken from the 'LNER East Coast Carriage Working, July 1939'.

The information indicates that the train left Glasgow at 9-25am and Edinburgh at 10-28. It consisted of seven coaches, five of which were going through to Harwich, and two Great Western vehicles to Southampton terminus. The Southampton brake third (in which the guard was to travel) conveyed luggage for Sheffield, Nottingham, Leicester, Rugby, Banbury, Oxford, Basingstoke, Winchester and Southampton. The coaches going to Harwich were LNER, ex-Great Eastern Railway stock, although one of the third class could have been a former North British vehicle. These had worked north the previous day from Parkeston Quay via York.

FROM	To	Vehicles in order from Engine.	Class.	Weight. Tons.	Seats. 1st.	Seats. 3rd.	DOWN WORKING
9.25 a.m. Glasgow to York		**(10.28 a.m. from Edinburgh)**					
(Saturdays, 8th July to 2nd September, inclusive.)							
Glasgow ...	Harwich ... (arr. 9.29 p.m.)	Brake Third	G.E.	28		18	7.25 a.m. from Parkeston Quay 3.35 p.m. from York.
		Third ...	G.E.	31		42	
		Compo ...	G.E.	30	12	27	
		Brake Compo	G.E.	34	12	24	
		Third ...	N.B.orG.E	31		42	7.33 a.m. from Southamp. ton Terminus. 3.35 p.m. from York.
	Southampton Terminus (arr.10.43p.m.)	Compo ...	G.W.	32	18	24	
		Brake Third	G W.	32		24	
Newcastle ... (dep. 1.0 p.m.)	Oxford ... (arr. 8.5 p.m.)	Rest. Compo	G W.	33	8	18	10.50 a.m. from Oxford. Empty by 3.10 a.m. M.X. 3.15 a.m. M.O. from York.
		Brake Third	G.W.	31		24	
	Swindon ... (arr. 10.8 p.m.)	Brake Van ...	G.W.	23			
	Leaving ,,	Edinburgh	...	218	42	201	
		Newcastle	...	305	42	225	
9.25 a.m. Glasgow to York, (10.28 a.m. from Edinburgh)							
Saturdays, 9th, 16th and 23rd September.							
Glasgow ...	York ... (arr. 2.40 p.m.)	Brake Third	N.B.	30		30	Locally.
		Compo ...	N.B.	32		12	
		Open Third ...	N.B.	32	30	48	
		Rest, Compo	N.B.	41		18	
		Third ...	N.B.	31	12	48	
		Third ...	N.B.	31		48	
		Brake Third	N.B.	28		18	
	Harwich ... (arr. 9.29 p.m.)	Brake Compo	G.E.	31	12	24	7.25 a.m. from Parkeston Quay 3.35 p.m. from York.
		Third	N.B. or G.E.	31		42	
	Southampton (Terminus) (arr.10.43 m.)	Compo	G.W.	32	18	24	7.33 a.m. from Southampton Terminus. 3.35 p.m. from York.
		Brake Third	G.W.	32		24	
Newcastle ...	Swindon ... (arr. 10.8 p.m.)	Brake Van ...	G.W.	23			Empty by 3.10 a.m. M.X. 3.15 a.m. M.O. from York.
	Leaving	Edinburgh ...	....	354	60	270	

Loading of Luggage, Parcels, Parcel Post, etc.
9.25 a.m. Glasgow to York (10.28 a.m. from Edinburgh)
Saturdays, 8th July to 2nd September inclusive.

HARWICH BRAKE THIRD.
Luggage for Harwich.

HARWICH BRAKE COMPO.
North End. Luggage and Parcels for Worksop, Lincoln, Spalding, March, Ely, Ipswich, Parkeston Quay.
South End. Luggage for Doncaster and Immingham Dock.

SOUTHAMPTON BRAKE THIRD (Guard).
Luggage for Sheffield, Nottingham, Leicester, Rugby, Banbury, Oxford, Basingstoke, Winchester and Southampton.

OXFORD BRAKE THIRD. Luggage for Oxford.
Note.—Parcels from Glasgow, Edinburgh, Berwick, Newcastle and Darlington for stations up to and including York and transfer to be forwarded by 7.44 a.m. from Glasgow and 10.40 a.m. from Edinburgh.

NEWCASTLE TO SWINDON G.W. VAN.
Rear End. Traffic for West of England viz. :—Taunton and transfer, Exeter, Newton Abbot, Plymouth and Cornish Stations.
Centre. Traffic for Swindon and transfer including Bath and Bristol, Westbury and Weymouth.
Front End. Traffic for South Wales Stations. No traffic for Banbury, Oxford and transfer to be loaded in this Van.

GENERAL PARCELS LOADING FROM :—   TO BE RESTRICTED TO :—

Edinburgh	
Berwick	York and beyond.
Newcastle	
Darlington	

9.25 a.m. Glasgow to York. (10.28 a.m. from Edinburgh)
Saturdays, 9th, 16th and 23rd Sept.

YORK BRAKE THIRDS.
Luggage for Berwick, Newcastle, Darlington and York.

HARWICH BRAKE COMPO.
North End. Luggage and Parcels for Worksop, Lincoln, Spalding, March, Ely, Ipswich, Parkeston Quay.
South End. Luggage for Doncaster and Immingham Dock.

SOUTHAMPTON BRAKE THIRD (Guard).
Luggage for Sheffield, Nottingham, Leicester, Rugby, Banbury, Oxford, Basingstoke, Winchester and Southampton.
Note. Parcels from Glasgow, Edinburgh, Berwick, Newcastle and Darlington for Stations up to and including York and transfer to be forwarded by 7.42 a.m. from Glasgow and 10.40 a.m. from Edinburgh.

NEWCASTLE TO SWINDON G.W. VAN.
Rear End. Traffic for West of England, viz. :—Taunton and transfer, Exeter, Newton Abbot, Plymouth and Cornish Stations.
Centre. Traffic for Swindon and transfer including Bath and Bristol, Westbury and Weymouth.
Front End. Traffic for South Wales Stations. No traffic for Banbury, Oxford and transfer to be loaded in this van.

GENERAL PARCELS LOADING FROM :—   TO BE RESTRICTED TO :—

Edinburgh	
Berwick	York and beyond.
Newcastle	

At Newcastle the train was 'strengthened' by the addition of a composite restaurant car, a brake third and a brake van, all Great Western stock, making a load then of 305 tons and offering a total of 42 first class seats and 225 for third class. The first two coaches were going to Oxford and the parcel van (which had travelled empty from York at 3-40am that morning) was for Swindon where it was due to arrive at 10-8pm. Notice how luggage and parcels for various places were allocated specific areas. Look also at how concisely the above information is translated into the carriage working.

The same train on the next three Saturdays was made up differently. See if you can interpret the information. For all these trains the working arrangements beyond York would be on a different diagram. This 9-25 train was only one series of movements out of thousands each day.

The Great Western Railway had a good variety of vans for carrying parcels, newspapers, milk in churns and mail. These became part of BR stock in 1948. This example has the framing on the inside but there were also outside framed vehicles. These vans could carry loads of up to fourteen tons. (J A Wells)

Parcels trains also had to be carefully co-ordinated and an example of this working is from September 1960. It shows parcels, luggage, letter mail, parcel post, and sausage traffic between Swindon and York. The vans were assembled at Swindon from Penzance and other starting points as shown, and would be remarshalled into other trains for Sheffield, Newcastle, Leeds and Edinburgh once the train reached York.

WEEKDAYS

Vehicles in order from Engine	From	To	Seats F	Seats S	Weight Tons	Loading of Vans Traffic for	Next Working
		4 (N.E. 488)					
9.40 p.m. SX (10.25 p.m. SO)		SWINDON TO YORK					
Formation leaving Banbury:—							
BG(669) (W.R.)	Penzance	Sheffield	—	—	20	To be grouped :—Leicester, Nottingham, Sheffield and N.E. Region	8.45 a.m., 6.30 a.m. SuO. Sheffield, Manchester L. Rd.
BG(665) (E.R.)	Bristol	Sheffield	—	—	24	To be grouped :—Sheffield transfer (including N.E. Region)	
BG (718)	Banbury	York	—	—	29	To be grouped :—Leicester, Nottingham, Sheffield, York	4.0 p.m. E.C.S. to Nottingham
BG (FSX) (720) (W.R.)	Calne....	York	—	—	20	Sausage traffic ex Messrs. Harris & Co.	10.22 p.m. (MSX) York to Calne
BG* (SX) (721)	Weymouth	Newcastle........	—	—	27	Messrs. Aplin & Barrett's traffic ex Yeovil	10.22 p.m. York to Swindon
BSK	Swindon	York	—	24	33	Luggage	10.22 p.m. York to Swindon
BCK	,, ...	(4.59 a.m. MX) (5.12 a.m. SuO)	12	24	33	Letter mails and luggage ...	
BG(W.R.) (728)	Paddington	York	—	—	20	To be grouped :—Rugby, Leicester, Nottingham and transfer, Sheffield and transfer, York, Darlington and Durham, Newcastle and Sunderland	6.40 p.m. York to Paddington
2 Vanfits B (510b) (SX)	Aylesbury (F) ...	,, ...	—	—	20	York, Newcastle, Edinburgh.	3.10 a.m. Dringhouses to Woodford Halse
BG(MX) (Sealed) (539a)	Leicester	Edinburgh	—	—	29	Glasgow, Edinburgh, York, Newcastle and transfer	
BZ (SX) (539)	,, ...	Leeds..............	—	—	13	Sheffield, Doncaster, Wakefield, Leeds	1.40 a.m. Leeds to Leicester
BG(SO) (541)	Nottingham	York	—	—	29	Doncaster, York, Darlington and Scottish.	
PMV (Locked) (SuO)(606)	Liverpool	Newcastle........	—	—	13	Newcastle, York	
BG(SuO) (621)	Manchester ...... (10.35 p.m.)	Newcastle........	—	—	29	To be grouped :—Newcastle, Durham, Darlington, Ferry-hill	
BG (SuO) (718)	Banbury .... (9.16 p.m.)	York	—	—	29	To be grouped :—York, Newcastle, Durham, Sunderland and Scottish	4.0 p.m. York to Nottingham Vic.
BG (SuO) (668)	West London ...	York	—	—	29	York and beyond	
PMV (731) Q(SuO)	Oxford	Newcastle ., ...	—	—	25	York and beyond Parcel Post	
BG(501)	Marylebone ...... (10.0 p.m.)	York	—	—	29	Parcels and Parcel Post for York and beyond	
No.of Vehicles							
8 (TO)	Arriving	Sheffield	12	48	248		
11 (WThFO)	,,	,,	12	48	277		
10 (SO)	,,	,,	12	48	257		
8 (SuO)			12	48	217		
	(E)—Attached at	Sheffield	W OR KS		3		
	(F)—Attached at	Woodford Halse					

(E) — to the row bracket spanning BG(SuO)(621), BG (SuO)(718), BG (SuO)(668), PMV(731) Q(SuO), BG(501)

(F) — Aylesbury (F)

Meaning of the abbreviations:-

BG ... Brake, gangwayed (i.e. with corridor connections)
BSK ... Brake second corridor
BCK ... Brake composite corridor
PMV ... Parcels and miscellaneous van
Vanfit ... 4-wheeled vans fitted with vacuum brakes
BZ ... 6-wheeled parcels van
WR ... Western Region
ER ... Eastern Region
FSX ... Fridays and Saturdays excepted
SX ... Saturdays excepted
MX ... Mondays excepted
SO ... Saturdays only
SuO ... Sundays only
Q ... Runs if required

To come right up to date, what about catering vehicles, which we expect to be part of trains travelling any distance? Below are three examples of rosters used by Virgin Trains to set you going:-

EXTRACTS FROM ROSTER FOR VIRGIN TRAINS' CATERING VEHICLES
(Two days in 2001)

Day One ... Catering car XC31
04-24   Derby EP to Sheffield
06-05   Sheffield – Birmingham
08-00   Birmingham – Manchester Pic.
10-16   Manchester Pic. – Birmingham
12-34   Birmingham – Manchester Pic.
15-36   Manchester Pic. – Birmingham Int'l.
18-47   Birmingham Int. – Liverpool

Day Two ...
08-10   Liverpool – Birmingham Int'l.
10-31   Birmingham Int'l. – Edinburgh
17-10   Edinburgh – Derby

Day One ... 158 Unit Catering car XC304 (Day Two same)
04-11   Tyseley – Cheltenham (empty)
05-30   Cheltenham – Swindon
07-04   Swindon – Cheltenham
 9-34   Cheltenham – Swindon
10-50   Swindon – Gloucester

11-43	Gloucester – Swindon
12-51	Swindon – Gloucester
13-44	Gloucester – Swindon
14-54	Swindon – Gloucester
15-45	Gloucester – Swindon
16-55	Swindon – Gloucester
17-47	Gloucester – Swindon
18-54	Swindon – Gloucester
19-59	Gloucester – Swindon
20-52	Swindon – Cheltenham
22-10	Cheltenham – Swindon
23-18	Swindon – Cheltenham
00-20	Cheltenham – Tyseley (empty)

Day One . . . 'Voyager' 220 Units . . . Catering cars XC524 and XC525

05-48	Longsight – Preston (empty)
06-47	Preston – Blackpool
07-35	Blackpool – Portsmouth
14-40	Portsmouth – Blackpool
21-04	Blackpool – Longsight (empty)

Day Two . . . Same working.

GOODS TRAFFIC

In previous chapters several references have been made to goods traffic and wagon types for handling different loads. These will suggest to readers possible areas of study and need not be repeated here.

This is an example of cantilever fulcrum wagons being used to spread the weight of a heavy load over more wheels. Special precautions have to be taken when the cargo is out-of-gauge. (Author's collection)

Going back to pre-Grouping days, each railway had its own ideas about design and construction, methods which in many cases had been tried and tested over many years. It can be interesting to compare different styles of, say, brake vans, and vehicles for carrying fish, fruit, livestock, coal and minerals, or milk, then trace how these were developed after Grouping. It is worth looking at the detail of buffers, couplings, brakes and wheels. The three-hole disc wheel was introduced in the mid-1930s but spoke wheels continued to find favour. It was not unusual to see one pair of each on a wagon, where one pair had to be replaced but a matching pair was unavailable.

Numerous types of freight wagons can be found on heritage railways, in museums, and on model railways. This is an ICI tanker for nitric acid, at the National Railway Museum in 1978. (J A Wells)

Mention has been made of marshalling yards, which were of two types, flat and humped. Trains arrived in reception sidings and were sorted by shunting engines. In flat yards a 'cut' of wagons would be nudged on their way. This was known as 'loose shunting' and as the wagons ran slowly into a particular 'road' their speed was controlled by shunters who ran alongside and applied hand brakes. Sometimes the wagons just banged into others already standing. Loose shunting should not be confused with 'fly shunting', which was used in some smaller goods yards as a way of saving shunting movements. It was different in that the engine was *ahead* of some wagons, in other words on the front of them. It gave a quick tug to get them moving, was then

It is worth looking closely at the detail of freight wagons. These are engineers' ballast tipping vehicles code named 'Dogfish'. They are fitted with heavy duty buffers and Instanter couplings which can be used in the long or short position (illustrated). The flexible pipes are for vacuum brakes. (J A Wells)

deftly uncoupled by the use of a shunting pole and ran quickly ahead onto one line. The trucks followed and when the points were changed, usually by a point lever beside them, they ran onto a different track. Provided the guard knew how to judge the speed of the engine and wagons, and when to throw over the lever, all was well!

In hump yards the train was pushed up a slope and the wagons, which had been uncoupled according to which line they had to go on, ran down the other side of the bank by gravity. In this way wagons were sorted for the next part of their journey and as each train was made up it was transferred to the departure sidings. The more modern yards were operated from a control tower from where points were changed electrically and the speed of wagons was controlled by retarders. Some wagons carried warning signs giving a message such as NO LOOSE SHUNTING, or a destination label clearly marked SHUNT WITH CARE.

The use of train ferries brought foreign stock to Britain but long, four-wheeled trucks built in this country gradually reflected continental standards. Now, because of the Channel Tunnel, stock from all over Europe can be seen and there are further opportunities for 'wagon-watchers' in the high capacity, bogie stock, undeniably of American style.

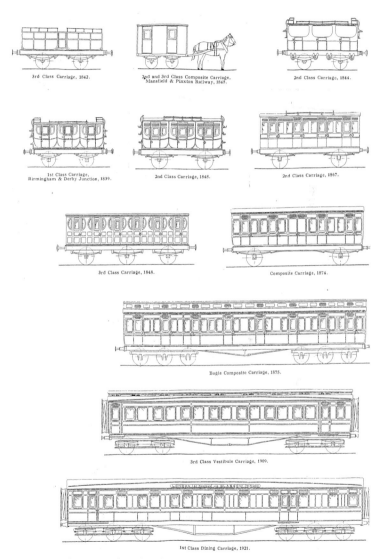

3rd Class Carriage, 1842.

2nd and 3rd Class Composite Carriage,
Mansfield & Pinxton Railway, 1848.

2nd Class Carriage, 1844.

1st Class Carriage,
Birmingham & Derby Junction, 1839.

2nd Class Carriage, 1848.

2nd Class Carriage, 1867.

3rd Class Carriage, 1848.

Composite Carriage, 1874.

Bogie Composite Carriage, 1875.

3rd Class Vestibule Carriage, 1909.

1st Class Dining Carriage, 1921.

*Diagrams showing the development of passenger carriages on the
Midland Railway. (Courtesy of the 'Railway Gazette')*

LONDON AND NORTH WESTERN RAILWAY.

ARRANGEMENT OF CARRIAGES

COMPOSING

HER MAJESTY'S TRAIN

From GOSPORT to BALLATER,

ON FRIDAY, THE 31ST AUGUST, AND SATURDAY, THE 1ST SEPTEMBER, 1900.

ENGINE.	VAN, No. 210.	CARRIAGE, No. 870.	SALOON, No. 72.	SALOON, No. 73.	SALOON, No. 153.	SALOON, No. 56.	SALOON, No. 50.	Royal Saloon.			SALOON, No. 131.	SALOON, No. 71.	SALOON, No. 130.	CARRIAGE, No. 306.	TRUCK, No. 100.	VAN, No. 272.
	GUARD.	For New Servants.	For Pages and Upper Servants.	Dressers and Ladies' Maids.	Dowager Lady Churchill, Hon. Harriet Phipps, Hon. Dorothy Vivian.	Princess Alexandra, Leopold, and Marquis of Battenberg, Mr. Theobald.	Princess Victoria Eugenie of Battenberg, Madame de Jaffa.	Queen's Dressers.	Her Majesty and Princess Henry of Battenberg.	Personal Servants.	Lieut.-Col. Davidson, Capt. Ponsonby, Sir James Reid, Bart.	Herr Von Pfyffer, Indian Attendants.	Directors.	Directors.	Forage. (To be attached at Basingstoke.)	Guard.

.... 326 feet 8 inches .... 269 feet 5 inches ....

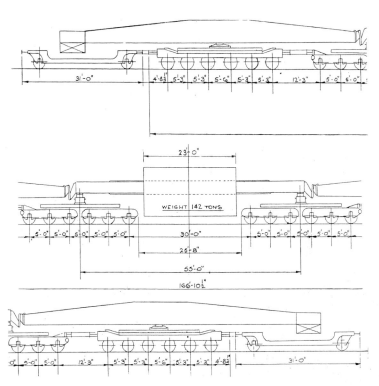

Where it was possible to support the weight of a heavy stator through the bore, the North Eastern Railway (and, later, the LNER and British Railways) used cantilever fulcrum wagons where the load was supported on 48 wheels. Balance weights at the extreme ends of the unit helped to take the weight from the centre vehicle. Speed was restricted, and engineers (travelling in an old coach) accompanied the train.

Chapter Seventeen
BUILDINGS, BRIDGES and SIGNALLING
ARCHITECTURE

We are very fortunate indeed that we have inherited from the Victorian era (1837-1901) a huge number of imposing station buildings. It was the coming of the railways that offered people the chance to travel much further afield with increased comfort. Railway companies engaged leading architects to design magnificent structures – often likened to cathedrals – with high, arched roofs dwarfing the trains they covered. They produced extravagant styles to reflect the importance of major stations in those days and these were landmarks in their towns and cities. John Dobson followed the classical style for Newcastle, an unprecedented design which came to be repeated all over the world. This station was opened in 1850 but was extended at various times. York has one of the finest roofs anywhere; designed by Thomas Prosser, it has three great arches of glass and iron covering platforms on long, sweeping curves. At Huddersfield the neo-classical edifice is flanked by Corinthian-style colonnades.

The present terminus at Paddington was built in 1854 and covered 70 acres. The length was nearly 800 feet, spanned by three semi-elliptical roofs. In the early days there were twelve miles of running lines and 38 miles of sidings within the first $1^1/2$ miles of the terminus, giving a hint of the heavy traffic using the station even then. The gigantic roof at London St Pancras, 240 feet across and 100 feet above rail level, contained $2^1/2$ acres of glass and 9,000 tons of ironwork. 60 million bricks and 80,000 cubic feet of dressed stone were used in the construction of this Midland Railway terminus. These buildings, and many like them all over the country, were regarded as monuments, or marks of recognition, for the benefits the railways had brought, yet notable designs were also to be found in hundreds of smaller stations across the land.

Larger stations were built for passengers to join or alight from trains in safety; they were places where tickets could be bought and people could wait under cover for connections, meet families and friends, or even have a haircut. These stations gave out information and provided toilet facilities, but also offered places to eat, left luggage offices and lost property rooms. In addition, staff of all grades were accommodated in rooms or offices.

Passengers included those travelling to or from work, going on holiday, visiting places of interest, or travelling on business. We must not forget therefore railway hotels which formed an integral part of many stations.

The main entrance at London Waterloo is also a war memorial dedicated to those London & South Western Railway staff who were killed in World War I. Built of Portland stone, it is known as the Victory Arch. (J A Wells)

From the 1840s thousands of small or medium-sized stations were built, to be enlarged or altered later according to traffic demands. In general there would be a booking hall adjoining the booking office, a general waiting room and sometimes one for ladies only. There would be an area for receiving and despatching parcels, probably in the booking office itself. The station master would have his own office, perhaps the station inspector or foreman likewise. Often the platforms were covered, or partly covered, by a canopy to provide shelter from the elements.

Look carefully at any station and observe the number of through platforms and bays. Are they joined by a footbridge or by a subway? How is the canopy supported – by pillars, beams or brackets? Is there a distinctive style of architecture such as Gothic, Monastic or Tudor? What are the buildings constructed from? Is there a station master's house – if so is it attached to station buildings or does it stand alone? What about the warehouse or goods shed, and the signal box? Some companies provided very attractive premises even on quiet branch lines, whereas others erected basic, functional accommodation as cheaply as possible.

Apart from their architectural merits, stations can be looked at for the service they provided. There were junctions where people changed trains, seaside termini like Cromer in Norfolk and Paignton in Devon, ports such as Hull and Southampton where passengers transferred between trains and ships or ferries; stations serving race courses, and those provided for service personnel or factory workers.

Today vast amounts of money have been spent on stations like Leeds, Euston and Glasgow where alterations and refurbishment have revitalised them. Large stations now accommodate an assortment of restaurants and snack bars, shops and stalls for gifts, clothing, confectionery and fruit. It is also gratifying to see numerous stations presenting gorgeous displays of hanging baskets, tubs and containers, often done in staff's own time. There may be fewer station gardens these days but it shows there are still people who care about the station where they work.

BRIDGES AND VIADUCTS

For anyone interested in bridges and viaducts there are multitudes of them all over the British Isles. Larger bridges cross rivers and wider expanses of water; smaller ones take a railway over and under roads, other tracks, and canals. Viaducts, on the other hand, have a series of stone or brick arches across valleys and uneven ground, or are a means of raising the railway above houses and roadways. Seeing how engineers of the day overcame tremendous obstacles and difficulties is another subject worth considering.

Some of the bridges over the river Thames have remarkable features but so much unseen work is in the foundations. Everything had to be carefully calculated beforehand. To support the nine spans of Charing Cross bridge in London eighteen large cylinders had to be sunk through mud and gravel to depths of up to 70 feet before being filled with brickwork and concrete. Each one was then tested with weights of 700 tons, an amount equal to the proposed four tracks being filled with locomotives. Only then could construction of the superstructure commence. After three years' work, the bridge was opened in 1863.

For crossing the Thames at Maidenhead without interfering with river traffic, Isambard Kingdom Brunel designed a very flat but elegant bridge. As originally built, it had two semi-elliptical brick arches with spans of 130 feet and rising to 24 feet. These were supported by a central pier in the river. On land each side were much smaller semi-circular arches to cope with flood water. If the structure had been higher it would have meant quite steep gradients on either side, but the size of the main arches and their low height caused some people to question its strength and stability.

Robert Stephenson's Britannia bridge, opened in 1850, was designed with the object of carrying the heaviest trains of the time over the Menai Strait in defiance of the swirling storms characteristic of that area. The choice of rectangular, iron 'boxes' joined together and supported on three piers was the result of numerous experiments which were concluded when a one-sixth size scale model was tested and found to be totally satisfactory. Work on the actual bridge could then begin. Getting the 440-feet central spans – and similar massive sections on bridges else-where – into position taxed the ingenuity of the engineers, but they rose to the challenges, as F S Williams records. The tower in the middle of the strait, which rose to a height of 230 feet, was built from marble for the exterior and sandstone for the interior, strengthened by beams and girders to give a weight of more than 20,000 tons. The abutments at both ends of this colossal bridge featured two couchant lions, Egyptian style, each of the four weighing 80 tons and needing 2,000 cubic feet of limestone for its construction. Following a serious fire in May 1970, the tubes were replaced by arched girders.

By contrast Robert Stephenson's High Level bridge across the Tyne at Newcastle was preceded by a temporary wooden struc-ture that was brought into use at the end of August 1848. Incredibly, only a year later the completed bridge was passed by Government officials after thorough tests had been completed. This six-span bridge, which carries road traffic on a deck sus-pended below the railway, was opened by Queen Victoria on 28th September 1849 on her way back from Scotland. It was designed when loads would be no more than 100 tons but was subsequently used by trains ten times as heavy, and numerous lorries and buses. Latterly, Railtrack has imposed a weight restriction which means that steam locomotives and heavy freight trains are banned.

At Dundee the bridge over the Tay estuary on the main line between Edinburgh and Aberdeen is over two miles long. It was opened in 1887 to replace the original which had partly collapsed in gale force winds at the end of 1879. A passenger train had plunged into the turbulent waters below with the tragic loss of 78 lives. The locomotive was recovered and repaired but – according to legend – when the Scottish crews refused to drive it the engine was transferred to the North British shed at Reedsmouth in Northumberland where it was nicknamed The Dipper.

Perhaps the most awesome structure is the bridge over the Firth of Forth in Scotland which is the oldest example of a cantilever type. Designed by Benjamin Baker and John Fowler, it was opened in March 1890 and consists of three cantilever towers 340 feet high. It is estimated that 8 million rivets were used in the building of this bridge. Its total length is just over $1^1/2$ miles, overshadowing anything previously built, rather like comparing a newly born infant with a Guardsman. 4,600 men were employed when construction was at its height, but 57 were killed in the seven years it took to erect. Looking at a train 156 feet above high water mark running through these gigantic steel girders, it is minuscule!

For the construction of a viaduct a timber gantry was built either side of the work, wide enough for the piers and abutments to be built between. A crane, or jenny, was placed on a moveable platform extending from one side to the other. The materials were wound up from below by hand or steam power, moved slowly along and lowered into the exact position where needed. Stones of great size could be handled in this way. As the height of the masonry was built up, new timber was added, the crane was raised and the next phase continued.

The line constructed by the South Western Railway was built as a viaduct for nearly two miles from Nine Elms to Waterloo. By contrast, when the South Eastern Railway was being laid it was decided to erect a timber viaduct to carry the line between Shakespeare tunnel and the Arch Cliff Fort at Dover. After piles had been driven into the rock, a light, open framework supported the elevated platform on which the rails were laid. Timber, stone or bricks were used separately or together on many early viaducts, but eventually timber ones were replaced.

A trip by rail over the Settle & Carlisle route is an experience seldom forgotten. Acres of trees give way to huge expanses of remote moorland; and mountain regions contrast with quiet valleys. After heavy or prolonged rain, white-flecked streams bounce and cascade down rocky hillsides before vanishing into culverts beneath the track. Viaducts stride like stilt walkers across the valleys. In late summer Ribblehead offers breath-taking views across the heather clad moors where the railway is carried on 24 arches standing up to 165 feet from the bottom of the foundations to rail level. The line sweeps round to avoid the dominating Whernside range before plunging into Blea Moor tunnel. One can only marvel at the railway builders' achievements.

In connection with Saltburn's Victorian celebrations on Sunday 16 August 1987, 'Pacers' 143019/022 operated three charter trips on the freight-only line to Skinningrove. Here one such train from Saltburn is crossing Riftswood Viaduct. (Ian S Carr)

SIGNALLING

So far we have considered locomotives and rolling stock, architecture, bridges and viaducts as offering various possibilities for extending your interest in railways. We can also include signalling and railway safety as a further topic.

The oldest railways had very primitive signalling, if any at all. Colliery lines had little need for signals at first – it was all done visually. The principal object of a colliery railway system was to transport coal, but miners were also carried between groups of collieries and this led to passengers being allowed to use the trains.

On public railways basic safety procedures were quickly introduced, bearing in mind the limited knowledge available at first. Enter the railway policemen who controlled the movement of trains by coloured flags, lamps, or simply by using their arms. Different companies had their own ideas and fixed signals were gradually introduced. On one railway a red flag would be run up a post to denote danger – not much good if there was no wind; on another a lamp on a post could be partly rotated from below to show white for 'proceed' or red for 'stop'. Disc signals, circular boards about two feet in diameter, were used in places. Facing an approaching train they meant danger but when turned end-on it was the all clear signal. The word 'board' is still used frequently today to denote a signal. Semaphore signals appeared early on some railways. One type had three positions, namely horizontal (normally at right angles to the track), pointing down at an angle of about 45 degrees, or dropping into a slot in the post, out of sight. These indicated 'stop', 'proceed with caution', or 'all clear'. Semaphores were next controlled by wires from a convenient spot. When these were put under cover they became the first signal boxes. In the course of time, to give engine drivers advance warning of the signals ahead, distance signals were introduced, but the name was later changed to distant signals.

Let us move on to the 1950s to look at a typical small to medium signal box on a main line or branch, the type now replicated on preserved lines. Inside are coloured, metal levers coming through a black metal frame at floor level. These levers are connected by rods or wires to points and signals outside. Red ones control home signals; yellow, distant signals; black operate points through a series of cranks; blue are locking bars which have to be released before facing points can be changed; brown are used in connection with gate wheels and wicket gates; white levers are spare. Home signals protect points and crossings, and control the movement of trains on the main line, loops and sidings. The front of the arm is red with a vertical white band, the reverse is white with a corresponding black band. At night they show a red or green light. Signals facing away from the cabin show a small white light in the dark which confirms the lamp is lit. (Railwaymen in some parts call these 'back-boards'.) When a signal is in the all-clear position at night, this light is shielded and the signalman then knows the signal is 'off'. Distant signals, which have a fish-tail end, are yellow with a black angled piece following the shape of the 'tail'. The reverse is white, again with the chevron in black. These signals show a green or orange light at night.

Where signals are out of sight of the signalman dials in the signal box show ON for at danger, OFF for clear, or WRONG if the signal arm is not in the correct position of about 45 degrees. The tension of the wire can then be adjusted by the signalman. It is not possible for a distant signal to show clear if the home signals ahead are at danger.

On facing points, a locking device is incorporated to hold the blades firmly in position and signals cannot be cleared if points are not properly closed. Pieces of coal or a stone can jam points, so also can frost and snow, but these days many sets of points are fitted with heaters to prevent them from freezing up.

Above and behind the lever frame in the signal box hangs a large track diagram with every point and signal shown and numbered to correspond with the levers. Some signal box diagrams have track circuits that light up red when a train passes over the relevant sections of the track, and these lock signals in the rear at danger electrically.

Fixed above the frame is a stout shelf of polished wood on which are mainly block bells and block instruments. As with other equipment, the design of these varies from zone to zone. These are used to pass information about the control of trains from one signal cabin to others adjacent to it. It may be useful to have a very basic introduction as to how the block system works. Every route is divided into sections (sometimes called block sections), each of which is controlled by a signal box. The distance between them varies between a few hundred yards and some miles.

Imagine three signal boxes, A, B and C. At A, a passenger train which will call at all stations is waiting to depart along a branch line. As its booked time approaches the signalman there gives one beat on the block bell tapper which rings out in B. B replies, one beat. A then 'offers' the train by tapping out 3 pause 1, thereby asking, "Is your line clear for a stopping passenger train?" If the answer is to be "Yes, my line is clear", B repeats the code to A, 3-1, and turns the knob of his block instrument to Line Clear. His lower dial (see illustration) now points to Line Clear and the upper dial on the corresponding instrument in A does the same. Without this the home signal at A that controls entry into the section leading to B is locked electrically at dan-

*Essential equipment for the safe signalling of trains using the absolute
block system – the block instrument and the block bell. (J A Wells)*

ger. When the train leaves A the signalman gives two beats on the block bell to show it is entering the section towards B. B acknowledges this and turns his block instrument to show Train on Line. Again the lower dial shows the same, likewise the upper one in A. (The latter cannot now send another train forward until the passenger train has safely passed B.)

The signalman at B now rings one beat on the block bell to C, Call Attention. C replies and is offered 3-1. If his section of line is clear the code to B is repeated; if not he ignores it and B cannot pull off his signals even if he wanted to. This time all is well, there is no need to delay the train and B clears his signals. As the train passes him he gives two beats on the block bell to C, who in turn will pass it on to D, and so on. The signalman at B checks the train as it passes him, ensuring there are no carriage doors open, no-one yelling for help, and above all that there is a tail lamp on the last vehicle, which must be lit at night, and shows the train is complete. If everything is all right he returns his signals to danger, then going to his block bell, he calls the attention of A. A replies, one beat, and receives the Train Out of Section bell code, 2-1, which he repeats. Having sent this, B returns his block instrument to the Line Blocked position. (Remember, under this system, a section is assumed to be blocked until it is proved to be clear.) A can now offer another train if there is one to go.

There are different bell codes for each class of train, and to cover all eventualities. Here are some examples of bell codes:-

Is your line clear for . . .

An express passenger train or a breakdown train going to clear the line	4 beats
A light engine or one with no more than two brake vans attached	2-3
Empty coaching stock train	2-2-1
Freight or coal train	4-1
Express parcels, fish, meat, etc.	1-3-1
Obstruction. Danger.	6
Train or vehicles running away on right line	4-5-5

Every bell signal, given or received, is entered in the Train Register Book. Unusual events, for example cattle on the line, heavy snow falls, derailments, or equipment failure, are entered in the Occurrence Book. If any of these old records can be located they can add variety to your study; and rules, specific instruc tions and safety precautions relating to signalling are worth following up.

Under the floor of the signal box is where the interlocking is located, which prevents conflicting movements. Each cabin is equipped with a three-aspect hand-lamp; red, yellow, and green flags; emergency detonators, and telephones. In the 1950s some single-needle telegraph instruments survived, but not for much longer.

Perhaps these brief notes will help you to understand the bewildering world of railway signalling, particularly if you visit a heritage line and see it in operation. You may then wish to look at later developments like colour-light signals and the computer systems that now help to control the traffic on our railways.

Chapter Eighteen
SOME POSSIBLE COLLECTIONS

Numerous people have an urge to collect things. If railways are your interest there are several options open to you – but first you need to answer some questions:-

What do you want to collect and why?

Where will you keep what you acquire? Do you have the space?

Will you be able to display your collection?

What is it going to cost you?

Are you thinking in terms of investment for the future, or will you buy and sell?

Is it likely to cause friction within your family?

People collect because there are things that remind them of childhood interests when railways were all around them. They want souvenirs or mementoes which evoke feelings of nostalgia, or link them with family members who worked on the railway. When it was thought we would never see steam hauled trains again people wanted to remember the action by acquiring loco-motive nameplates, number plates or whistles. This quickly broadened to embrace all kinds of railwayana, particularly with company names or initials. In this category we find heavy cast iron notices warning against trespass, iron lamp posts, lamps of

Collecting small items of railwayana is very popular with railway enthusiasts. There is a wide choice available, illustrated here by a carriage key, whistle, file clip and a stamped spoon. (J A Wells)

These are examples of armbands. The one marked Porter would be given to a temporary member of staff for identification purposes. The Fireman badge would be worn by members of staff at large premises where they would have a team to deal with small fires, or assist the fire brigade. (J A Wells)

different kinds, signalling equipment, station clocks, signs, seats and numerous smaller items like wooden cash bowls, inkwells, armbands and track elevation plates. These are all very collectable and much sought after.

NORTH EASTERN RAILWAY
PUBLIC WARNING
PERSONS ARE WARNED NOT TO TRESPASS
ON THIS RAILWAY, OR ON ANY OF THE
LINES, STATIONS, WORKS, OR PREMISES
CONNECTED THEREWITH.
ANY PERSON SO TRESPASSING IS LIABLE
TO A PENALTY OF FORTY SHILLINGS.
C. N. WILKINSON
SECRETARY.

MIDLAND RAILWAY.
7 VICT. CAP. 18 SEC. 238 ENACTS "THAT IF ANY
"PERSON SHALL BE OR TRAVEL OR PASS UPON FOOT
"UPON THE MIDLAND RAILWAY WITHOUT THE
"LICENSE AND CONSENT OF THE MIDLAND RAILWAY
"COMPANY, EVERY PERSON SO OFFENDING SHALL
"FORFEIT AND PAY ANY SUM NOT EXCEEDING TEN
"POUNDS FOR EVERY SUCH OFFENCE."
NOTICE IS THEREFORE HEREBY GIVEN THAT ALL
PERSONS FOUND TRESPASSING UPON THIS RAILWAY
OR THE WORKS THEREOF WILL BE PROSECUTED.
JUNE 1906.   ALEXIS L. CHARLES.
                           SECRETARY.

LONDON & NORTH EASTERN RAILWAY
WARNING TO TRESPASSERS
THE LONDON & NORTH EASTERN RAILWAY COMPANY
HEREBY GIVE WARNING TO ALL PERSONS NOT TO
TRESPASS UPON ANY OF THE RAILWAYS, STATIONS,
WORKS, LANDS OR PROPERTY BELONGING TO OR
WORKED BY THE COMPANY. TRESPASSERS ARE
LIABLE TO A FINE OR IMPRISONMENT FOR EVERY
OFFENCE.   BY ORDER

Heavy cast iron notices warning against trespass were a feature of railways well into the British Railway era. These are examples from the North Eastern Railway, the Midland Railway and the LNER. A fine of 40 shillings (£2) was a lot of money in those days – but a £10 fine must have been a fortune to most people. (J A Wells)

BOOKS. Many hundreds of railway books have been published from the earliest days and each year sees more and more produced, covering every possible aspect. Some people who like to buy new issues have large collections. Others are quite happy to purchase second hand, particularly books which interest them but which have been out of print for many years. There is a tremendous choice of books available from dealers, second hand bookshops and jumble sales, but do not overlook those that have been withdrawn from library stock and are offered for sale at a very low price.

BUILDERS' PLATES. These metal plates come in an assortment of shapes – rectangular, circular, triangular, oval, kidney-shaped, and more stylish designs. They were fixed to locomotives, tenders, coach underframes, wagon solebars and mobile cranes or track vehicles. The information given would, as a general rule, show the builder, the place built, the year, and a works or registered number. Signal gantries often had a fairly substantial plate showing the manufacturer – McKenzie & Holland being one of the main suppliers. People who collect metal plates may also include other plates showing wagon codes or their designated use such as 'Grampus' (an Engineers' wagon), 'Fish', 'Meat', 'Gunpowder', etc. where they are used as an alternative to paint. There are also plates for special instructions, limitations or restrictions.

BUTTONS & BADGES. Most railway companies included on their uniforms brass or silver coloured buttons bearing the company's initials or a miniature crest based on their coat of arms. Badges were sometimes used to denote the rank of, say, foreman or station master, and were worn on the lapel or cap. These buttons and badges were continued by British Railways in various forms.

CARRIAGE PRINTS. It was a common practice at one time, particularly when coaches had separate compartments, to display prints behind glass, below the luggage racks. There would be up to six in each compartment, about eighteen inches long and eight inches wide to fit neatly into the frames. Apart from adding a little décor, they would have the effect of silently suggesting to passengers places to visit as they day-dreamed about having a day away by train, or a holiday. The subjects did vary but many featured a train in attractive surroundings. A series in colour by the railway artist C Hamilton Ellis depicted rail travel in various eras, all of which were historically correct.

Builder's plate from LNER brake van.

Mckenzie & Holland plates could be seen on signal gantries or lever frames in signal boxes.

Less common are plates from vans forming part of NER breakdown trains built from 1889 to 1900. (J A Wells)

CHINA & CUTLERY. The days of good china and cutlery bearing the name or initials of the company from pre-Grouping or post-Grouping days have long gone, but they still appear in sales or auctions and are hastily snapped up by collectors. In the 1960s sets of china cups, saucers and plates, with milk jug and sugar basin, showing well known steam locomotives were produced to raise funds for railway orphanages. More recently, locomotives have featured on collectors' plates by various manufactures.

CIGARETTE CARDS. Tobacco companies have issued many thousands of cigarette cards since the 1920s. These are very collectable and auctions or fairs are held regularly. Murray Cards (International) Ltd has reprinted Cartophilic Society reference books. Railways have been well covered especially by W A & A C Churchman, W D & H O Wills and R & J Hill Ltd. The latter produced five series commemorating the Stockton & Darlington Railway Centenary in 1925. Tea companies, the Co-operative Wholesale Society Ltd., a laundry, chewing gum manufacturers, and 'The Scout' magazine of 1924 were just some of the alternative sources of cards. Subjects covered have included locomotives, famous trains, landmarks in railway progress, rail travel, railway history, preserved railway locomotives (1983-84), and railway equipment. A clean set of cards illustrating Railway Posters by Famous Artists, issued in 1930, was worth an estimated £350 in 1998.

CRESTS. Although full size transfers of railway crests are obtainable it is not easy to apply them and it requires some expertise to do so. Smaller, mounted versions are available from some larger museums or railway centres. For railway modelling purposes, however, crest transfers for different railway companies are available. Expert modellers can create their own with the help of a computer.

This subject is one which is ideal for photography, being relatively cheap, accessible, and quite easily stored using slides or prints. Alternatively, close-up shots of crests on locomotives or coaches can add an extra feature when a video camera is being used.

EPITAPHS. Gravestones have honoured men who worked all their life on the railway or who died following a railway accident. Memorials and inscriptions can offer sincere and heartfelt tributes to former colleagues, and were often printed in newspapers and magazines as the following example shows:-

In Memory of
HERBERT TAPLEY
(Late Guard N.E.Railway)
who was killed in a dreadful collision
at Brockley Whinns
on December the 6th 1870
Aged 26 years

Come, Railway-Men, in grief lament,
Another solemn warning's sent!
One of our band, we held most dear,
Is done with time, and all things here.
Young Tapley was a man complete;
In all his actions, just, discreet;
No pride had he, nor vain presuming!
But modest, kind, and unassuming.
His duties always well performed;
In person clean, and neat adorn'd;
To be polite, he ne'er neglected;
And was by all loved and respected.
How deep our grief; how sad the blow
That laid our young companion low!
One moment well; oh, hapless case!
The next he's found in Death's embrace,
Strange providence; true to thy trust;
The good and kind thou tak'st first;
No more, while steaming through the air,
He'll guard his train with anxious care;
Ah; no, the Chariots up on high,
Meet no obstructions in the sky!
No fatal points to lead astray,
Nor turn them in a dubious way!
Safe, safe, we hope out friend is there,
Protected by Almighty care.

A FELLOW SERVANT
10th Dec. 1870

This topic is very much on the fringe of possible collections but it has been the subject of talks.

INN SIGNS. This is a wide ranging and popular subject for talks and articles in magazines – but going round to photograph pub names and signs must be as good an excuse as any for visiting a different hostelry! Some ordinary names like 'The Railway', 'The Station', and 'The Locomotive' appear all over. You can add to these the public houses named after a particular railway, like 'The Blyth & Tyne', and to subjects with a railway connection like 'The Porter', 'The Grand Junction', 'The Atmospheric Railway' or 'The Lickey Banker'. In the north east, the home of railways, we find 'The George Stephenson', though nearby 'The Rocket' has been renamed. Inevitably, there is the 'Flying Scotsman' alongside the east coast main line.

Some of the illustrations are excellent but, sad to say, there are others which are hopelessly inadequate, a distorted hotchpotch. Parts of locomotives that are difficult to illustrate – like the valve gear – are simply smothered in steam by the artist. Even then they are worth photographing if only to show how not to paint a railway engine!

LUGGAGE LABELS. Stations used to keep stocks of coloured labels for principal destinations of luggage, and sometimes parcels. These were glued on and made the handling of the items quicker and easier for those involved, rather than having to scrutinize address labels. Passengers travelling on important expresses like the 'Coronation' were often given a special label advertising the train, which could be pasted on their suitcase or trunk.

MODEL RAILWAYS. As mentioned elsewhere, railway modelling is a very popular hobby for children and adults. Rolling stock, track, equipment and accessories can be bought new, second hand, given as a gift, or exchanged. In time a very creditable system can be built up and the operating of the layout can give a great deal of pleasure. On the other hand a lot of people are happy just to keep their locomotives and stock boxed and unused as a long-term investment. Their satisfaction lies in having a look at them from time to time and just knowing they are there. Mint and boxed models always command a much higher price if they are to be sold.

PHOTOGRAPHS. You must decide whether you want to build up a collection of your own material over a period of years – but what do you do if the subjects you want are no longer available? In that case you can buy prints or slides taken by others provided they are not used as your own or for personal gain without permission. There is usually no harm in cutting pictures out of magazines or newspapers for a personal scrapbook.

POSTAGE STAMPS. The Post Office has issued occasional stamps with a railway theme, mainly to commemorate notable events like the opening of the Channel Tunnel, or anniversaries such as the Liverpool & Manchester Railway 150. Philatelic companies have at times produced specific envelopes for use with these stamps. In addition there are railway preservation groups which have their own stamps and envelopes to mark so many years of progress or the return to steam of a certain locomotive. Some collectors prefer to concentrate on first-day covers only, whereas others widen the field by including stamps from abroad which illustrate British railway history or achievements.

POSTCARDS. For railway enthusiasts who love to comb through boxes of old postcards it is always an extra thrill to find one written many years before, probably from a soldier in World War I to his folks back home, saying, ". . . I changed trains at this station on my way to . . ." It may have been kept locked away in a house somewhere until, eventually, it ended up in a sale. Stations, junctions, locomotives, the latest in rail travel, special records, major

This postcard shows the first electric passenger train, introduced by the North Eastern Railway in 1904 – but it was not long before a new version was produced. (Author's collection)

events, railway accidents, bridges, cartoons poking fun at the railway – they are all there on old postcards. When electric trains were introduced on Tyneside in 1904 they were very popular but a cartoonist portrayed one arriving at a station on the Never Early Railway so full that passengers were hanging on outside or trying to wriggle through windows, packed on the roof (even reading a newspaper), and scrambling into the driver's cab. He did not forget to include dead dogs and electrocuted cats! More modern cards of steam, diesel and electric trains are available in some bookshops, station bookstalls and card shops.

POSTERS. This is a very wide subject because railway companies have used posters in numerous sizes to catch the eye of passengers. Travel by rail, places to visit, special excursions, continental connections, timetables, facilities for freight, overnight travel by 'sleeper', and station closures are just some of the subjects, but we must not forget warnings about trespass and vandalism. In centres like the National Railway Museum some miniature-size replicas are available.

TICKETS. The first railway tickets were actually coloured or white paper on which details of the journey were hand written, a rather slow process. At Milton station, on the Newcastle & Carlisle Railway, Thomas Edmundson devised a system of using cardboard tickets he had previously printed himself and numbered in sequence by hand. These were kept in special racks. The numbers enabled him to know how many tickets had been issued to the various stations and he was able to check that the money he had taken was correct. The company adopted this system for all its stations. In 1837 he brought into use a ticket dating press, the principle of which was used throughout the railway system to the 1950s. Naturally, covering such a long period, there are tickets from pre-Grouping days, the Big Four, British Railways, Privatisation and the Underground, not forgetting, of course, heritage railways. The types of ticket include singles, day returns; monthly, quarterly or longer periods; excursions, officials' passes, travel for members of the forces and platform tickets. Runabout tickets gave unlimited travel over a designated area for a period.

TRACK DIAGRAMS. The sort of track diagram you collect will depend on whether you are seeking to record layouts on a particular main line or branch at a given time or era, or whether you

want ideas for a model railway based on the prototype. Sizes vary from a convenient A4 to full-size signal box diagrams.
VIDEO CAMERAS. This is more of building up your own collection rather than acquiring something over a period. You film what interests you, and after editing you can enjoy the results of your labours whenever you want to do so on your television.

_____

The very condensed information in this chapter is to give you some idea of the scope available – after all 'Railways' is a very diverse subject, which is why it appeals to so many people. So, where can you find what you are looking for? You can join a group dedicated to your special interest; buy, exchange or be given what is no longer of use to someone else; or visit specialist auctions, exhibitions, jumble sales, car boot sales and the like. Whatever you choose, your hobby should bring you many happy hours.

British Rail used to have a centre at Euston known as 'Collectors' Corner', for unwanted railway material. This was later transferred to York but has now closed. Nevertheless, many of the objects which originated from there are still in circulation.

Finally, a word about prices. It seems that records at auctions continue to be broken frequently, particularly for locomotive nameplates which can bring bids of £40,000 or more for the genuine article.

A poster of an A3 in silhouette advertising the 'Night Scotsman' train in 1931 brought £1,000. Prices range from £500 to £4,000, depending on condition, the artist, date, and so on. Carriage prints can bring up to £500 in mint condition. Clocks from stations, signal boxes and offices were worth up to £1,000 in 2001. Prices of smokebox number plates reflect the class of engine, with prestigious locomotives bringing much higher amounts. Even a builder's plate from a locomotive can cost several thousand pounds. Wagon plates are very common – hence much cheaper – unless it is a rare pre-Grouping item. For lamps of various kinds prices would start at about £50.

Some very good quality replicas of nameplates, number plates, etc. are available but care should be taken that these are not mistaken for the real thing. In these days when there is no incentive to save because of very poor returns, more and more people are investing in railwayana. Those who bought items from BR for what would now be considered ridiculously low prices have seen their investments increase abundantly. Nevertheless, be warned, *PRICES CAN ALSO FALL!*

This book has attempted to show the fascination and sheer variety of railways. No other country has the legacy we have inherited. Our records of railway history are the envy of the world; and the extent of our heritage lines is unsurpassed. Schemes are in hand to open even more branch lines and to restore more locomotives and stock. All over the country groups are making available their research for our benefit, ably supplemented by excellent magazines. Every day there is an explosion of information on the Internet. It is all there for you to enjoy – but there is also a place for you if you would like to help with restoration, preservation, operation or research. Enjoy it!

MIDLAND RAILWAY

COOK'S CHEAP EXCURSION

DURHAM, NEWCASTLE, AND BERWICK.

A CHEAP EXCURSION TRAIN WILL RUN

FROM LONDON

(ST. PANCRAS STATION), BY THE MIDLAND RAILWAY COMPANY'S ROUTE,

On **TUESDAY, JUNE 29th, 1880,**

AS FOLLOWS:—

				FROM St. Pancras or Kentish Town.		FROM Watling Street, Aldersgate Street, or Farringdon Street.	
				Third Class.	First Class.	Third Class.	First Class.
				s. d.	s. d.	s. d.	s. d.
NORTHALLERTON RICHMOND DARLINGTON	...	...	...	17 6	35 0	18 0	35 6
DURHAM NEWCASTLE	...	...	...	20 0	40 0	20 6	40 6
BERWICK	...	...	...	25 0	50 0	25 6	50 6

Returning on WEDNESDAY, JULY 7th, as follows:—

				P.M.				
From BERWICK	...	at	4 5	From DARLINGTON	...	at	8 18
„ NEWCASTLE	...	„	7 8	„ RICHMOND	...	„	6 25
„ DURHAM	...	„	7 5	„ NORTHALLERTON	...	„	8 41
LONDON (St. Pancras)	...	arr.	4 15 m	LONDON (St. Pancras)	...	arr.	4 15 a.m.

Children under Three years of age, Free; above Three and under Twelve, Half Fares. Tickets are not Transferable, and only a limited quantity of Luggage allowed, under the Passengers' own care, for which the Company will not be responsible.

TICKETS may be obtained on the two previous days to the running of the Train, at the MIDLAND BOOKING OFFICE, St. Pancras Station; at the Tourist Office, in front of St. Pancras Station; at the Midland Office, 445, West Strand (opposite Charing Cross Station and Hotel); at 13, Aldersgate Street; at 272, Regent Circus, Oxford Street; at COOK'S TOURIST OFFICES, Ludgate Circus, Fleet Street; and on the day of the running of the Train, at the Stations only. An early application for them is particularly requested.

Derby, June, 1880.

JOHN NOBLE, General Manager.

For full particulars of above, and of all Cook's Excursions and Tours to the Midland District, and all parts of the Continent; also of Special Tours and Single Journey Through Tickets to all parts of the UNITED STATES and CANADA, apply to

THOS. COOK & SON,

Chief Office—Ludgate Circus, London.   Euston Road Office—In Front of St. West-End Agency—445, West Strand   Pancras Station. Crystal Palace Tourist Court.

Thos. Cook & Son, Ludgate Circus, London.

Many documents are not in good condition, partly due to poor storage or rough handling. Even then they often contain invaluable information. (Darlington Railway Centre and Museum)

BRITISH RAILWAYS

1949 F.A. CUP—FINAL TIE—
WOLVERHAMPTON WANDERERS v LEICESTER CITY
1st Division Championship—
SUNDERLAND v CHELSEA at STAMFORD BRIDGE

EXCURSION TO

Wembley
for the Cup Final

with Bookings to London
FRIDAY NIGHT 29th APRIL

OUTWARD		Third return fare to Wembley or King's Cross		RETURN	
	p.m.	s.	d.		p.m.
†MONKSEATON ....dep.	10 29	57	0	KING'S CROSS ....dep	11 20 (30th)
†WHITLEY BAY .... ,,	10 31	57	0		a.m.
†TYNEMOUTH................... ,,	10 36	57	0	YORK ....arr.	3 26 May 1st
†NORTH SHIELDS .... ,,	10 39	56	10	**THORNABY .... ,,	5 45
†WALLSEND .... ,,	10 47	56	2	**MIDDLESBROUGH ...... ,,	5 51
NEWCASTLE .... ,,	11 30	55	3	‡SOUTH BANK .... ,,	7 3
PELAW........................... ,,	11 39	54	1	§REDCAR .... ,,	7 20
•JARROW .... ,,	11 26	54	9	§SALTBURN .... ,,	7 34
•HEBBURN .... ,,	11 30	54	6	STOCKTON .... ,,	4 42
‡SOUTH SHIELDS .... ,,	10 44	55	0	BILLINGHAM .... ,,	4 56
‡TYNE DOCK .... ,,	10 51	54	8	WEST HARTLEPOOL ...... ,,	5 12
SUNDERLAND .... ,,	11 55	53	6	HORDEN .... ,,	5 31
	a.m.			EASINGTON .... ,,	5 38
SEAHAM .... ,,	12 5 (30th)	53	6	SEAHAM .... ,,	5 48
EASINGTON .... ,,	12 14	52	2	SUNDERLAND................ ,,	6 5
HORDEN .... ,,	12 19	51	10	‡TYNE DOCK .... ,,	6 48
WEST HARTLEPOOL .... ,,	12 31	50	6	‡SOUTH SHIELDS .... ,,	6 53
BILLINGHAM .... ,,	12 45	48	10	PELAW .... ,,	6 22
STOCKTON .... ,,	12 59	48	1	•HEBBURN .... ,,	6 40
**SALTBURN .... ,,	10 43	51	3	•JARROW .... ,,	6 42
**REDCAR .... ,,	10 56	50	5	NEWCASTLE .... ,	6 36
**SOUTH BANK .... ,,	11 7	49	3	†WALLSEND .... ,,	7 10
**MIDDLESBROUGH .... ,,	11 15	48	8	†NORTH SHIELDS .... ,,	7 17
**THORNABY .... ,,	11 22	48	1	†TYNEMOUTH .... ,,	7 20
YORK .... ,,	2 15	38	4	†WHITLEY BAY .... ,,	7 25
KING'S CROSS ....arr.	6 30			†MONKSEATON .... ,,	7 27

† Change at Newcastle   • Change at Pelaw   ** Change at Stockton
‡ Change at Sunderland on the Outward journey and Pelaw on Return
§ Change at Stockton and Middlesbrough

THROUGH EXCURSION BOOKINGS TO WEMBLEY

Passengers find their own way at own expense between King's Cross and Marylebone : a special service of trains will run between Marylebone and the Wembley Stadium Station commencing at 12·0 noon, the journey occupying 14 minutes
After the match a frequent service of trains will be run from the Stadium Station to Marylebone. Marylebone Station can be easily reached from King's Cross either by Electric Train or Motor Bus
In the event of the Match being cancelled or postponed this special train will not run provided the Railway Executive receive notice at the station of departure in sufficient time to cancel the arrangements

TICKETS CAN BE OBTAINED IN ADVANCE

Further information will be supplied on application to the stations, agencies, or to the District Passenger Manager, British Railways—Newcastle, Tel. 20741.

CONDITIONS OF ISSUE

These tickets are issued subject to the conditions of issue of ordinary passenger tickets where applicable and also to the special conditions as set out in the Bye Laws, Regulations and Conditions in the Public Notices of the Railway Executive
Luggage Allowances are set out in the General Notices
Children under three years of age free ; three years and under fourteen, half-fares

A typical handbill advertising a special trip to London for the 1949 FA Cup Final. (Darlington Railway Centre and Museum)

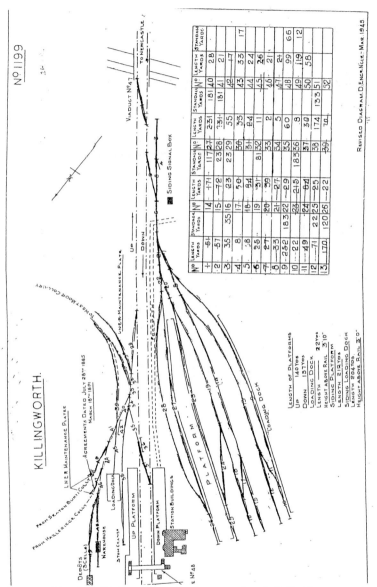

An example of a district engineer's diagram dated 1945. They come in various sizes and were well used. On this one some of the lines had been over-drawn in red or blue pencil at some time in the past, probably when tracks were to be removed. The island platform and sidings were used for races traffic but now only main lines remain.

L.N.E.R.

_____ Station.

B. 794

Return of*_____ Salvage collected and brought to debit through the Balance Sheet as Compensation—(Salvage).

Month ended _____ 19

Date Paid in	Reference to correspondence of Station	Reference to correspondence of Manager or District Officer	Amount Collected £ s. d.	REMARKS

Est. 4642. 100,000. 9/36

O. 6924

LONDON & NORTH EASTERN RAILWAY.

EMPTY COACHING STOCK.

FROM... TO.....................................

VIA...

No. and type of Vehicles..

*Required for use..

Per instructions from...

Date...
* This line need only

LNER 8507/11/38 5,000 pads of 250

B. 1150

L.N.E.R.

From ....

_To_ ....

Telephone No. ;

193

Paperwork

L.N.E.R.

G. 523

ENQUIRY FOR MISSING GOODS

From...

....

Ref..   ....194....

Invoice No.......................From...................................To...............................

Date.........................Wagon No....................Consignee..................................

Full description of ⎫
goods, number of ⎬ ....
packages and marks ⎭ ....

Weight...Dimensions....................................

THE ABOVE GOODS ARE MISSING. HAVE YOU ANY TRACE ?

To..   Signature..............................

....

Labels

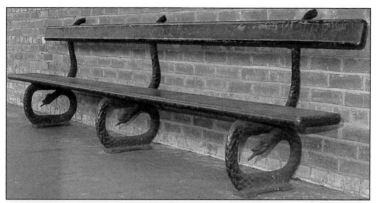

Some people like to acquire photographs which show how things used to be in the past. Illustrated here are a snake seat (with broken tails), a point lever for changing points by hand and one bogie of a former Great Central Railway boiler wagon.

The National Railway Museum's replica of **Rocket** *has visited many events, where it is always a popular performer. An open day at Didcot is the location for this photograph. (K Morton)*

Timothy Hackworth's **Sans Pareil** *may not have won the Rainhill trials but it was a useful locomotive on the Liverpool & Manchester Railway in the early days. The replica appears from time to time on preserved railways. (K Morton)*

Part of the fascinating display of Underground trains at Acton Museum which also features London Transport buses. (J A Wells)

*Bressingham is the home of this beautifully restored narrow gauge locomotive number 1643 **Bronllwyd** which was rescued from a slate quarry in Wales. (K Morton)*

*One of the 'Tilbury tanks', 4-4-2T **Thundersley** is resident at Bressingham, Norfolk. It was built by the London Tilbury & Southend railway for express work. (K Morton)*

An unusual exhibit in the National Railway Museum is this seat from the Furness Railway. (J A Wells)

*A view of Didcot Railway Centre, home of the Great Western Society. Castle Class number 5051 **Drysllwyn Castle** and Prairie tank number 6106 are shown. (J A Wells)*

*Having brought in the empty stock of 'The North Yorkshireman' Pullman dining train, 34101 **Hartland** is running round its train prior to an evening departure on the North Yorkshire Moors Railway, May 1998.*

(J A Wells)

Flying Scotsman, the world's most famous steam locomotive, at speed on the east coast main line, prior to electrification. After its overhaul, the engine now has a double chimney and German-style smoke deflectors.

(J A Wells)

*Former LMS Pacific number 46229 **Duchess of Hamilton** on a charter train at Carlisle in 1998. This locomotive is in the national collection.*

(K Morton)

A different form of charter train was 'Steam on the Met,' in which four steam engines worked trains between Amersham and Watford, either singly or double headed. B12 4-6-0 61572 leaves Rickmansworth in May 2000. This locomotive is based on the North Norfolk Railway. (J A Wells)

Contrasting liveries of two class 37 diesels hauling a charter of maroon stock. The leading locomotive is 37428 in colours to match the 'Royal Scotsman' tour train. (K Morton)

The Deltic Preservation Society, owners of 50017, chose to paint their class 50 locomotive in an LMS style of red and gold. It is seen with a 'Northern Belle' charter at Carlisle. (K Morton)

The NER built some vans that had part of the roof made from canvas so that heavy objects could be handled with the help of a crane. This feature has been captured on this detailed 7mm scale model hand-built by George Mitcheson. (G.R. Mitcheson)

Lion *was the oldest working locomotive when it ran before an excited crowd at Rainhill in 1979. It was the 'star' of the film 'The Titfield Thunderbolt'. (K Morton)*

Various aspects of railway archaeology can be found at Manchester Victoria, a principal station of the Lancashire & Yorkshire Railway. The large wall route map was still there in 2001. (J A Wells)

A train to promote Mars products has toured the country, giving the company widespread publicity. Normally based at Bounds Green, London, it is shown heading to Scotland on the east coast main line in September 1997. The locomotive on this occasion was 47677 advertising 'Celebrations'. (J A Wells)

Like many Victorian locomotives, the 'Stirling single', with its pair of huge driving wheels, is an elegant machine capable of fast speeds. It is sometimes steamed for special occasions and has visited some heritage lines.

The J72 0-6-0 tank engines were built by the North Eastern, the LNER and British Railways. 69023 worked as station pilot (shunter) at Newcastle for some years, hence the NER/LNER livery and crests of the North Eastern and British Railways. Although based on the North Yorkshire Moors Railway, it is loaned to other heritage railways. (K Morton)

It is sometimes necessary to make light engine movements when locomotives are required for special trains. Volunteers in the support crew helped with watering, pushing coal forward, and checking lubrication when **Britannia** paused at Garsdale on the Settle & Carlisle route in 1991. (J A Wells)

Rail express sysetms. Class 47

*Former Southern Railway
'Merchant Navy' class.*

GNER. 125 power Car

Virgin 125 power car.

*Class 47 diesel.
A selection of locomotive
nameplates. (J A Wells)*

*Former Southern Railway West
Country class.*

*HM The Queen visited Newcastle to celebrate the 150th Anniversary of the Central Station. The Royal Train is seen arriving on 7 December 2000, hauled by 67005 **Queen's Messenger** which she had named at Euston the previous evening. (J A Wells)*

Settle, a typical Midland Railway rural station on the Settle & Carlisle route. (J A Wells)

Part of the former Lancashire & Yorkshire Railway station at Halifax, a listed building no longer used for railway purposes. Notice the attractive Yorkshire stone with which it was constructed. (J A Wells)

From the 1960s Newcastle signal box was a Route Relay Interlocking Colour-light system in which points and signals were power operated and controlled by switches operated by the signalmen. White strips of lights showed which route had been set up, and the movements of trains were indicated by red lights on the diagram. The desk in the foreground was used by the duty controller. (J A Wells).

*On charter work, preserved class 46, **Ixion**, is framed by the lattice girder signal gantry at Scarborough with its array of home and shunting signals. (K Morton)*

*A few miles south of the England/Scotland border, the Royal Border Bridge
takes the east coast main line across the river Tweed at Berwick.*

(K Morton)

*Preserved Southern Railway 4-6-0 number 777 **Sir Lamiel** (King Arthur
class) makes a fine sight as it crosses Dent Head viaduct on the Settle &
Carlisle line. (K Morton).*

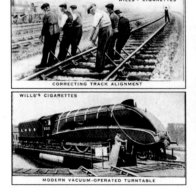

*Cigarette cards were issued by a number of tobacco companies and were
very popular. Today they are collectors' items. Four are illustrated.*

(J A Wells)

This very attractive poster by Herbert Truman was used by the Great Western Railway to advertise St Ives as a holiday resort.

(K Morton collection).

Coats of arms and crests make a colourful and interesting study for which a detailed knowledge of heraldry is not essential. This is a selection.
a) Great Western Railway; b) London & North Western; c) BR circular badge for coaches; d) Pullman; e) Caledonian; f) London Midland & Scottish; g) North Eastern; h) South East & Chatham. (J A Wells)

PHOTOGRAPHS BY SUBJECT

INDEX

BIBLIOGRAPHY

Boulton, W H   The Railways of Britain
Sampson Low, London, 1950

Deith, C L (Ed.)   Steam Heritage Museums & Rally Guide
Tee Publishing, 2000

Harris, Nigel & Holley, Mel (Eds.)
Steel Wheels – British Railways 1825 – 2000
E M A P Active

Horsefield, Brenda (Ed.)
Steam Horse: Iron Road
BBC 1972

Marshall, John   The Guinness Book of Rail Facts & Feats (2nd Ed.)
Guinness Superlatives Ltd., 1975

Richards, Tom (compiler)
Was Your Grandfather a Railwayman?
(3rd Ed.)
Published by the author and the
Federation of Family History Societies

Wells, J A   Blyth & Tyne Part I – The Blyth & Tyne Railway
Northumberland County Library, 1989
(Out of Print)

Williams, Frederick S
Our Iron Roads (3rd Ed.) 1883
Bemrose & Sons, London

The Railway Handbook 1939-40
The Railway Publishing Co. Ltd. 1939

ADDENDUM

Parts of this book have reflected the railway scene at the beginning of the 21st century, but things move on and it is appropriate to look at some recent developments up to the first quarter of 2003.

Network Rail is now shown to be a private sector company whose basic function is to efficiently operate, maintain and renew the railway infrastructure, working closely with the Strategic Rail Authority and having its efficiency monitored by the Office of the Rail Regulator. There are no shareholders and any profit made will be reinvested in the railway.

Work is continuing to renew track and update signalling in various parts of the country. London Euston and Leeds are two of the places which have been completely remodelled, but an on-going major project is the total modernisation of the west coast main line between Euston and Glasgow, parts of which have to be completely closed for varying periods. One section of fifty miles is to be shut down for four months. It is grossly over the original budget and modifications to the plans have meant that the proposed speed of tilting Pendolino trains (140mph) has had to be cut back to 125mph.

Stage One of the advancing Channel Tunnel Rail Link has now had the overhead line equipment switched on and will open for traffic in September 2003, meanwhile the mammoth task of fitting the Train Protection & Warning System across the rail network is virtually complete. This £500 million scheme aims to reduce considerably the dangers when signals are passed at danger (SPADs).

Passenger numbers have continued to grow significantly, but this has led to overcrowding in many places. Train operators have placed large orders for new stock and these are being brought into service throughout the country. First Great Western introduced 'Adelante' stock in June 2002; new trains are at work in Scotland, and South West Trains expect huge additions to their stock. Several other companies are spending millions of pounds refurbishing their stock to higher standards – GNER is an example. New, colourful liveries advertise companies' trains. Midland Mainline has decided to change from the popular teal green to ocean blue and silver. The eye-catching Virgin Voyagers and Super Voyagers (those with tilting capabilities), 76 sets in total, are in regular service on CrossCountry routes, but these shorter trains of four or five coaches create problems even though there are more of them. If two sets are combined the number of on-board staff, apart from the driver, has to be doubled as it is not possible to pass from one unit to the other because of their streamlined ends. The longest run in March 2003 continues to be between Dundee and Penzance, 700 miles. Virgin Pendolinos are already appearing on main lines on the west side of the country. Eurostar trains ran though to Avignon on eight summer Saturdays in 2002, in preparation for a new service.

In contrast were the disruption and frequent cancellations of freight trains through the Channel Tunnel, caused by would-be immigrants seeking to use them as a means of entering the UK illegally.

The order by EWS for 250 class 66 locomotives from General Motors, Canada, was completed promptly but was followed by orders from other freight groups, notably Freightliner (who will have over 40 of the class), GB Freight and Direct Rail Services. At the end of the 1990s, some class 37s were used in France on construction work for a high speed line; now fourteen of the class have been painted blue and hired for four years to work in Spain on similar duties. Prior to the withdrawal of 47-hauled passenger trains, Virgin painted four of the class in earlier BR liveries and used them on various services, a gesture appreciated by enthusiasts. Class 86 number E3172 was returned to the 1960s electric blue livery. In an attempt to reduce trespass and vandalism, Virgin also painted 47829 to look like a Police car. This too took its turn on service trains. ["What a cop" as the train spotters would have said!]

Steam specials on the main line have produced some spectacular runs – and some disappointments. The former LMS Pacific number 6233 Duchess of Sutherland is back after a £400,000 overhaul and had the honour of hauling the Royal Train for part of HM The Queen's Golden Jubilee Royal Tour of 2002. Also returned after nine years is 6201 Princess Elizabeth; and almost ready for the main line is 71000 Duke of Gloucester. The Gresley V2 60800 Green Arrow continues to give reliable performances, and in due course we shall see Royal Scot and Lord Nelson at the head of charters. There are of course others, but, on heritage lines also, progress and satisfaction go hand in hand as long-term projects reach completion.

It is worth recording that in a re-run of the Rainhill Trials for a television programme, the replica Rocket again triumphed over its competitors Sans Pareil and Novelty.

This is just a glimpse at what is happening on Britain's iron roads, but as a result of more trains running on already congested tracks, the SRA has ordered changes to be made from when the summer and autumn timetables are introduced in May and September 2002. Train services will be reduced or altered to cut down delays!